# SEX,
## LOVE,
### *and*
## DHARMA

**ALSO BY ARTHUR JEON**

*City Dharma:*
*Keeping Your Cool in the Chaos*

# SEX, LOVE, and DHARMA

## FINDING LOVE WITHOUT LOSING YOUR WAY

### Arthur Jeon

THREE RIVERS PRESS
NEW YORK

Three Rivers Press and the Tugboat design are registered
trademarks of Random House, Inc.

Library of Congress Cataloging-in-Publication Data
Jeon, Arthur.
    Sex, love, and dharma : finding love without losing your way /
Arthur Jeon.—1st ed.
    1. Love—Religious aspects—Buddhism.  2. Interpersonal
relations—Religious aspects—Buddhism.  I. Title.
BQ4570.L6J46 2004
294.3'444—dc22          2004028613

ISBN 1-4000-4910-5

Printed in the United States of America

Design by Trella Mendl Design Group Inc.

10 9 8 7 6 5 4 3 2 1

First Edition

For the women who have taught me so much about romantic love, with all its passions, joys, and illusions.

Especially SG, KM, WP, ML, and JG.

I couldn't have written this book without you!

# ACKNOWLEDGMENTS

I thought writing a second book on the dharma would be easier than writing the first. Boy, was I wrong! In some ways it was much harder. The topic took me to places I hadn't traveled in my own heart and forced me to look at things unseen up to now in my own life. It could not have been written without substantial support from many different people.

To Catherine Ingram, who first introduced me to the dharma, thank you.

My family has continued to provide unstinting love and support. I am grateful and lucky to have them behind me in my wandering creative journey.

To all my friends who have been sounding boards for the book, sometimes without even knowing it, including Helena Kriel, Lea Russo, Devin Whatley, Andy Stern, Oliver Butcher, Joel Fields, and Eric Freiser, thank you. You are like family, and all those conversations over the years about the nature of love and reality have informed my thinking and made their way into the book.

Julia Pastore, my editor, you really are a saint. You have nudged me along, kept me focused, and given great feedback in a gentle and persuasive way. Truly, you have been a partner in the creation of the book and very patient with my challenging questions.

Special thanks to Shaye Areheart and the rest of the team at Harmony/Three Rivers Press, including my publicists, Darlene Faster, Selina Cicogna, and Paige Alexander, and the design team for both book covers. The whole experience was so easy in the hands of such competence. Thank you for standing by me for both books.

Thank you again to my agent, Eileen Cope, for your guidance and support, and for getting me the deal that allowed me the luxury of writing two books about the dharma. What a privilege you made possible! A fond thank you to Linda Loewenthal, who first brought the books into Harmony.

Finally, to my lovers throughout my life—no matter how it ended, I have loved you all, you have taught me much, and I remember you all with deep love. Thank you.

With love,

Arthur Jeon

# CONTENTS

# SEX,
## LOVE,
### *and*
## DHARMA

# INTRODUCTION

Sweet Love say
Where, how and when
What do you want of me? . . .
Yours I am, for you I was born:
What do you want of me?

SAINT TERESA OF AVILA

Recently I was hiking in the Santa Monica Mountains on a sunny Sunday morning. I was with a friend and we were moving fast, passing other people walking in pairs up the trail. The snatches of conversation were different, but all had a similar theme.

"He's just so . . . I don't know . . . he gets quiet and I don't know what he's thinking," said one woman to another.

"She's a total drama queen," puffed a guy on a bike to his friend.

". . . and then I said, if you don't like my friends, just stay home."

"He looks right through me. We haven't had sex in a month!"

And so it went as we hiked up the mountain. Every single couple, whether male or female, was talking about their relationships. They weren't talking about work or family or geopolitics; they were talking about their partners.

And most of the conversations didn't sound happy.

As men and women grope for ways to be with each other, as gay men and woman redefine love and family, there are a lot of questions about what, exactly, love is. In a time when the divorce rate is at fifty percent, what is left of the institution of marriage? How do we navigate our natural biological gender differences with compassion and understanding?

Some people have sworn off relationships entirely. Some are caught up in idealized visions of romantic love, the one person in the world who will make it all perfect for them. People in dramatic, difficult relationships rationalize their difficulties with talk of relationships as a way to work out their "issues." Others look at partnerships as a spiritual journey toward discovering the love within them. Some think relationships should last forever; others feel that serial monogamy is the only paradigm that makes sense.

One thing everybody seems to agree on is that relationships are difficult. Ultimately it feels as if there are as many definitions of partnership as there are people on the planet. Within this diversity, are there certain immutable truths? How does one have a nuts-and-bolts working relationship while exploring deeper spiritual yearnings? Are the two mutually exclusive?

As I wrote the chapter on relationships in my last book, *City Dharma,* it kept growing and growing. Ironically, while it was the chapter that was the greatest challenge for me to write, it was also the one that seemed to hold my interest the most. I found myself wanting to add more pages and go deeper into the issues I was exploring. Instead, I began taking notes on issues relating to love that I didn't have room for in *City Dharma,* knowing during the last year that I was going to write the second book on love and relationships, from the first hello to the final good-bye, whether that good-bye is in a divorce or on a deathbed.

*Dharma,* which means "the way" or "the path," is from a Sanskrit word for the essential character or nature of all that is. It refers to the principle or energy that orders the universe. It is both *why* things are as they are and the *path* to the realization of why things are as they are. It refers to waking up from our own conditioning and way of seeing the world.

When I contemplated writing *Sex, Love, and Dharma,* I wanted to apply the principles of wakefulness to romantic relationship. How can you see another human being clearly as they really are, rather than as you'd like them to be? How do you avoid the traps of repeatedly choosing the same unavailable person over and over again? How do you keep your own conditioning from causing you to destroy your relationship? Is there a way to experience unlimited love even when you are not with a partner? Is it possible to love a person when you don't like certain parts of their personality?

As Marcel Proust said, "The real voyage of discovery consists not in seeing new landscapes, but in having new eyes." This is the core of what *Sex, Love, and Dharma* is about—seeing the world of love differently. When you are in the dharma, you are not identified with your thoughts, your ego, or your conditioning, and you begin to see reality clearly, without filters. You become free of the mind, which makes a wonderful servant but a terrible master. You begin to see the world *as it is* rather than *as you want it to be;* you see it without the crazy-making obscuration of a mind run amok with habitual thought. You see potential partners clearly, without the obscuration of projection. Steeped in the dharma, lacking identification with *me, me, me,* you experience yourself as an integral part of all that is, and out of this comes complete freedom. You feel connection rather than separation, and love rather than fear. You are awake and able to experience joy and happiness that is independent of externals.

Along with addressing the constant fears and stories generated by the mind when involved in relationship, *Sex, Love, and Dharma* posits the radical claim that freedom and true love are available in the here and now, no matter what the circumstances. In fact, this freedom is only available in the present moment and, conversely, the present moment is actually your portal into this freedom—it is a life raft on the stormy sea of mind, which is usually in full flight from love. Full absorption in the present moment is a way to leach out the nattering of the mind and ego, which are always concerned with the past and the future. But all we really have is the present moment; the future never comes and the past is gone and dead. Right now is the only *livable moment,* and the only time in which love can truly flourish. Once this awareness is stabilized, love is its natural offspring.

I also wanted to write a book that was real and gritty

and wasn't overtly precious or "spiritual," whatever that ultimately means—for in the dharma, it's all spiritual. The stories, for better or worse, are true and look at all sides of the question of love, from the darkest shadow to the brightest light. I hope to show a way of looking at love differently, not by outlining any spiritual "practice," because what are you practicing *for*? You can't say I'm going to feel love at *x* moment in the future, once I've practiced for it. Love can only be felt right now, in the moment. Ultimately, this book is about completely restructuring the way you look at love.

Although there are many profound psychological principles in *Sex, Love, and Dharma,* it is not another psychologically based book about "getting the love you deserve." In fact, this notion is questioned right from the start. While I integrate the psychology of personality, I move beyond it, for psychology without spirituality ultimately goes nowhere. At the end of the day, one's "story," after it is understood and dissected, must be dropped. What *Sex, Love, and Dharma* will do is help you to identify and drop your story, help you to see reality more clearly, with fresh eyes. It is in the awareness of the dharma that we are all much more likely to find love without losing our way.

This book is not Buddhist, although it could be called Buddhism without the beliefs. The teachings upon which this book is based are called Advaita Vedanta, ancient teachings based in the Vedic texts, and they offer no religious handrails, nor do they ask you to believe in any fairy tales, instead concentrating on the ultimate realization that all is consciousness. Although there are different manifestations of consciousness, it is all one blast. And from this awareness there can be no loneliness, no fear, and no loss.

Again, it is a *way of seeing* rather than the acquiring of techniques or belief systems. *Sex, Love, and Dharma,* at the heart of the matter, posits the idea you are already awake and all you need to do is realize it. There is a famous Zen quote: "When you wake up, the world wakes up around you." In this spirit, the book will portray ways in which we all fall asleep and in which we all can wake up to true love, rather than wallowing in ego-based transactional love.

Mind you, I am not writing this book as an expert on love. I am just a fellow traveler on the path. Many of my friends are single. Some are married. Some are divorced. In addition to innumerable stories I have heard in my weekly Dharma Conversations, I have a reservoir of stories to draw from, including my own experience. Again, all of them are true, although all the names have been changed.

When I told a friend of mine that my second book after *City Dharma* was a book about applying the dharma to relationships, she laughed cynically.

"That is the biggest joke I've ever heard."

"Why?" I asked. But I already knew why. I'm single and live alone with my cat. My relationship history has been long and varied, with more drama than most theaters.

"Because you know absolutely nothing about the subject of love," she said, confirming my suspicions.

"Gee, don't hold back."

"Well, you've had how many relationships?"

"Uh . . . a lot, and your point is?"

"You can't teach what you don't know."

Ouch. Although sometimes I think that with friends like this, who needs enemies, it's a legitimate point. I haven't been married for thirty years, with all that entails in terms of love, sacrifice, and forgiveness. I don't have children, with what all that means in terms of the above, plus large doses of patience.

In fact, I have made every possible mistake regarding relationships. I have chosen badly, behaved badly, created messes with fine women, while hopelessly chasing the mirage of unavailable women. I have had expectations, been arrogant and stubborn and insensitive. I have been caught up in my own needs and ideas about romantic love. I have been wrong many, many times. And to those of you who have had an actual direct experience with me when I was at my least conscious, I'm sure you can think of some more specific things I did wrong. I've sincerely and personally apologized to everybody I've hurt, but let me do so again here. I'm sorry.

I am a full human being, warts and all. So who better to write a book about love? Somebody with no experience? Somebody who married the first person they met? Somebody who hasn't seen every kind of relationship and screwed-up situation? It is precisely because I am not a saint that I feel my experience is useful. I have suffered in love and made others suffer. And the nondualistic teachings of Advaita Vedanta have ended that suffering.

So, in *Sex, Love, and Dharma* we will explore partnership in all its forms and challenges, starting before the projections of the first meeting and ending with the sadness of the last good-bye and including the jealousy, obsession, and craziness in between. We will look at what love means within the nondualistic spiritual teachings, in which nothing is alien, nothing is separate, and all is part of the one. The book is both a continuation of *City Dharma* and a deeper look at the greatest force driving mankind, the desire for enduring love. It addresses, too, the spiritual question of why having a "love of humanity" sometimes seems easier than being able to love one particular person well.

Although this book makes no promises about finding true love, it will help you figure out how to have more freedom and more love within the partnerships you do create, so that the tone and tenor of the conversation can finally begin to change as we trudge up the mountain together, communicating with each other instead of complaining about each other.

# PART ONE

# Way Before

## First There Was Aloneness

# LOVE

## Here's Looking at You, Kid

Get over your Self and simply love.
Drop yourself and love.
You are your Partner
Your Lover is You
You are your Lover

ANONYMOUS

We all search for love. We want it. We think it will make us whole. We think that we can finally be happy if we can find the love we desire.

We all make the mistake of looking outside of ourselves for that love, looking for somebody who will fulfill our every need and fantasy. We seek that external love and then completely forget to *express* love in our daily interactions.

Spiritually speaking, we get confused between the false love of the ego, which flows from a mindset of scarcity and need, and the love that comes from knowing one is part of the Divine in the universe and thus can never be empty of Love, *because love is what we are*. We are looking at it all the time.

Sounds good, you might be saying, but what the heck does that mean?

There is an old parable about a young bird that has just learned how to fly. The bird swoops and swirls and spins and flies. When it gets back to its nest, it has some questions for its mother.

"Mother, what's this stuff called 'air'? Everybody keeps talking about it. They say it's everywhere, but I can't see it anywhere."

This is exactly the way we are when we are searching for love rather than expressing it, when we are looking for "the one" rather than being "at one" with all we encounter. Because the currency of love is available all the time, supporting everything that we do, every single moment is an opportunity to give love, tapping into the flow of it. Don't look for it, for you *are* it.

There is a cashier at my local Wild Oats market who embodies this way of being. Her name is Reisha and she is a large woman, with natural warmth that slows you down, creating a hiccup in your impatience to get through the line. The other day I was waiting for her to ring me up and we were chatting. I started out in a hurry, but just being in her presence relaxed me.

"How are you today?" Reisha asked me with a welcoming smile.

"Good," I replied. "How are you?"

"You're looking at it," she said, smiling, unknowingly quoting a David Mamet line from his movie *Heist*. Or maybe she'd seen the movie. Regardless, her response was filled with a rueful knowing about life's ups and downs.

When the young person bagging my few items started to put the ripe peaches into the bottom of the bag, followed by heavier items, including a half-gallon of milk, Reisha gently stopped him.

"Okay now," she said patiently, pulling the items out of the bag. "This is the way you want to do it so the peaches don't get squished."

"Oh . . ." The young man was embarrassed by not getting something so simple right.

"Don't worry, you'll be fine once you get the system," Reisha said.

"Thanks," he said.

With that, Reisha turned to me and rang up the items before turning to the woman behind me, who had been watching the whole scene impatiently. Reisha smiled at the woman.

"How are you today?"

"Fine," said the woman. "And you?"

"You're looking at it," Reisha said. The woman loosened up and smiled in spite of herself.

Reisha was at it again, expressing warmth and love to one person at a time. She wasn't asking for anything. She didn't have anything to give except her presence. She was in a job most people would find beneath them. And yet she was expressing love, instead of searching for it.

In your life, in the smallest interactions with everybody you meet, there is an opportunity to *express* love. This way of being in the world changes the flow of energy between you and the rest of the world. It changes a dynamic of "not enough" into an outflow of "more than enough"—in fact, so much that here's some for you. And the more you exercise this expression of love, the more it grows.

This is because love is a verb. If we believe that love is a noun, then we think that it can be traded, given, withheld, sought after, possessed, and lost. If, on the other hand, we know love as a verb, giving or receiving it is ultimately the same, and love is both inexhaustible and infinite. As the Persian poet Rumi said, "Only from the heart can you touch the sky."

This is not dependent upon finding that special one person. When you feel you need somebody special in order to express love, you are ultimately weakened—you see yourself as dependent on other people as the source of love. This is a setup for disappointment and suffering. And anytime they don't meet your needs in the time, place, or manner you desire, in your disappointment you may try to seduce, cajole, manipulate, control, attack, or even kill that person. This is just the spectrum of human response to loss. Most of the time it doesn't escalate into violence, but often it does; we have all seen or even experienced physically or emotionally abusive relationships. The perpetrators of this violence, besides reenacting what they experienced as children, are trying to keep from losing their source of love, their "love supplier." But what they don't realize is that *they are this source.*

Right now, understand that *you are the source of the love you feel,* and nobody else. And the anxiety caused by the loss of that love is also yours.

In this awareness that you are love, you don't make anybody special, you make *everybody* special. Express your love to the world, in a sense making everybody your soul mate.

Then the question isn't where you go to "get the love that you deserve," because you don't have to go anywhere or to anybody. Just simply unblock your own heart and let it flow to everybody you encounter.

Love is energy. If you hoard it, it stagnates. If you let it flow, you begin to realize its inexhaustible nature.

# SELF-LOVE

## Dance Alone First, Attract a Partner Later

*You yourself,*
*as much as anybody*
*in the entire universe,*
*deserve your love and affection.*

BUDDHA

You can't learn to love another person until you've learned to love yourself—to say this is to tumble into the land of cliché. We've all heard it a million times from friends and therapists. But what does it mean to love oneself? Who is the self that you love? What does it look like? Where do you find it?

What happens when you ask the question, Who am I?

What comes to mind? Are you your education, your family, your job, your relationship, your likes and dislikes? On the level of personality, you are all of these things. But is "loving yourself" just a matter of loving your personality? What is underneath it? What is our true nature, which supports all of these aspects of personality?

As an exercise, keep asking yourself, Who am I?

Well, I am me, you might respond.

Okay. Who is that?

Well, I'm the son or daughter of my parents. I went to this school. Red is my favorite color. I like chocolate more than vanilla.

I am ME!!!!!!!

But, underneath it all, who or what is there?

Our society exults in the myth of the individual, from the original cowboys to presidents who pretend to be cowboys. We are all encouraged to be unique individuals, to let our individuality out. Tied to this is the idea that we must love ourselves. On the level of personality, this is true. Self-acceptance and self-love are necessary to healthy relationships. But on a truly spiritual level, the "I" disappears. There is no "I" to love. There is no story of "me."

There is simply *beingness.*

For instance, my friend Larry had a great job working in an entertainment company. It gave him prestige and lots of money and he fell into the trap of *identifying* with it, drawing his identity from this job. He started to feel as if he were synonymous with his work. Then the company downsized and he lost this job. Larry, a very talented person, spiraled out of control. He fell into a deep, almost suicidal depression. He couldn't get out of bed. This phenomenon happens a lot to men who retire, to the point where many actually die shortly afterward. This is what happens when you draw your identity from *doing* something rather than from simply *being.*

And this is true not only of work but of your relationships, your beliefs, and even your thoughts. True freedom means not identifying with anything.

Even now, as you read these words, try to drop your identification with what the mind is thinking. You do not draw your *identity* from your thoughts. Right now, even as you read these words, you are *reading,* but you are not a *reader.* In conversation, you are *listening,* but you are not a *listener.* When performing a task, you are *doing,* but you are not a *doer.* And when in relationship, you are *loving,* but you are not a *lover.* "You" disappear.

And in this simple beingness is freedom: freedom from identification with "me." And from this beingness comes the possibility of connecting with all that is. When you lose your identification with the small self, with all of its wants and needs, there is no barrier to experiencing a connection to the SELF—to all that is. The more strongly you are identified with "I" and "me," the more isolated and separated you feel; the more you feel the need to "get" the love you deserve. The less identified you are, the more connected you feel, and out of this comes a love that is connected to all things. It is not ego-based, but is actually a spiritual love.

This sounds so easy, but how do we do it? How do we drop our identification with jobs and money and success and partners in order to wake up? How do you feel love if you are chronically single? It is not really a matter of doing anything, for you are already there. It is important to know that you are already enlightened, and that all you need to do is to realize it, to drop the obscuration that prevents you from realizing this. It's sort of like asking, "How do I become a human being?" You *are* one.

But how do I realize it? How do I drop my identification with thought?

Simply by being fully present in each moment. If you bring your attention into this moment, right now, you can't think about anything else. You can't obsess about the past and you can't worry about the future. The identification and thoughts evaporate in the vibrancy of *right now*. The small self, with all its attendant thoughts and worries, disappears.

This makes it possible to see reality without the filter of desire and conditioning.

But what does waking up have to do with the expression of love? How does it affect it? What does spiritual love mean on the level of personality, especially if you are not identified with this personality?

It means that you are not driven by needs and desires. You just *are*.

Erich Fromm, in his classic book *The Art of Loving,* talks about the difference between immature and mature love. Immature love says, "I love you because I need you," while mature love says, "I need you because I love you." Fromm goes on to say, "Mature love is a state of productiveness which implies care, respect, responsibility, and knowledge. . . . It is an active striving for the growth and happiness of the loved person, rooted in one's own capacity to love." His definition says nothing about barter, conditions, seeking, or expectations, but focuses solely on caring for the other person.

In *Sex, Love, and Dharma,* we will look at love from many different angles.

**True love is different from material love.** True love is not about the experience of "falling in love" or infatuation.

Falling head over heels, being swept away—these feelings indicate a state of being ungrounded, as if a force has severed you from your sanity. This is all about the love chemicals that get released in the brain, along with large dollops of projection and desire. Relationship that begins with our need for the other person's love is doomed to fail unless it matures into spiritual love that is beyond infatuation.

**True love is not about anointing somebody as special.** To do so sets the trap of expectation. If they are "special" (i.e., worthy of our love), then they must continue to be special instead of who they really are. As soon as they lose their "specialness," the gloss goes off the relationship and you become dissatisfied. They have disappointed you by being human, with flaws and faults all their own. True love gives love to everybody it encounters. False love only gives it to those who are "special."

**True love is a verb.** You cannot experience what it is "to walk" or "to eat" without actually doing the actions of walking and eating. The same is true for "to love." Most people, however, treat love as a noun, an object that can be felt, bought, attained, bartered, and lost. Rather than looking to give love without expectation in return, we are always looking to get love, as if it were a precious and limited commodity.

**True love is not controlling.** When we are operating from ego-based love, there is a fear of autonomy in the other person. If they are too free, they might leave, right? So we try to manipulate and control their feelings and behavior. The flip side of this is that true love is not afraid of being controlled or engulfed—it has faith in the feelings that arise. True love lets people be who they are; it allows for trust that they can have their own life, friends, interests, and jobs and still love to be in relationship with us.

**True love doesn't need the other person to be glued to your hip in order to feel the love.** The emptiness we feel when we're not with our lover is due to the false sense of separateness. In the awareness of being joined together in one blast of consciousness, you feel your lover's presence even when they are not with you. In addition to their being in your heart and you in theirs, they are both connected to the energy of the universe (what Carl Jung called the collective unconscious). This is not just a concept; quantum physics has started to prove the connectedness of all things. This love survives all losses, even the loss from death.

**True love is not consumed with worry and fear.** Sometimes we worry about the person we love; it's natural and human. But this is based on a fear of losing the other person, whether to another person, disease, or death. In true love, there is no fear of that. We accept the impermanence of all things and express love without fear of loss.

**True love is most available when you don't identify with the "small self."** The more invisible you become to yourself, the more you drop your identification with the story of "me" and "what I think," then the more you are able to feel true love. This is because you are not relating everything back to how it affects you. You're not worried about the loss of love to you, because when you don't identify with your perception of yourself, "you" aren't there. You don't have any expectations, because you have seen through the illusion of a personality always asking "What's in it for me?" This leaves room for simply loving, without an agenda.

**With true love, you let go of all ideas of self-improvement.**

This may seem funny, coming from a so-called spiritual self-help book, but it points to our endless reworking of our personality. But what do you want to do, rearrange deck chairs on the *Titanic*? Do you want to get into the endless game of self-improvement, changing the different layers of conditioning, when the real task at hand is to allow them to dissolve? It's much more effective to take a sword to the Gordian Knot of Self than to try to untangle it strand by strand as your life passes you by.

Ultimately, there is nothing you need to do to improve yourself. You're fine exactly the way you are, because *you are not your personality*. You are pure consciousness, an integral part of the whole. Once you drop your identification with your small self, you realize your clear and present awareness. It's like hosing the mud off a window; the mud is the conditioned personality, the glass underneath it and supporting it is your true nature. You don't rearrange the mud of the small self, you simply let it fall away. In this recognition lies freedom and the opportunity to express love moment to moment.

This may be counterintuitive. It may contradict every "self-help" book that you've read. But the point is there is no "self" to help. So it is the opposite of the "change yourself and get the love you deserve" approach. It's more of a "drop yourself and simply love" approach. Ironically, although it is no reason to pursue the dharma, this way of being is so attractive to others, you will be a magnet for many potential partners who want to be around this freedom, and the compassion and generosity it generates.

For in this awareness comes the peace and confidence that love can never be lost. It is a part of you and thus a part of all that is.

# CONDITIONING

## You're Not Who You Think You Are

*Wisdom is knowing I am nothing, love is knowing I am everything, and between the two, my life moves.*

NISARGADATTA MAHARAJ

The other day, while I was heading to the beach with my friend Roberta, I caught a glimpse of a woman slamming the back door of her SUV shut. I couldn't see more of what was happening because she was blocked by another car, but I could feel her anger.

When we drove up to the woman, she opened the side door of the SUV and started hitting and screaming at a small boy in a child's seat. The child was wailing, and his little sister, also in a child's seat, was screaming hysterically. The woman's husband was getting out of the car on the passenger's side.

"What are you doing?" I said, raising my voice to the woman. "Stop that!"

The woman stopped smacking her kid.

"Get in the car!" the woman screamed at her husband, who was pulling the little girl out of the SUV. "They want the parking space!"

"I don't want the space," I said loudly. "I want you to stop hitting your kid."

"We're having a marital dispute, so now is not the best time." The woman, dressed in shorts and a halter top, her face tight with rage, glared at us. Her husband, who didn't say a word, was pulling the screaming boy out of the car. He seemed to be in control of the children, and they were safe from the woman for the moment, so I drove up and made a U-turn, heading back down the street toward the Pacific Coast Highway and the beach.

"That makes me feel sick," Roberta said. "I feel sick."

"Yeah," I said. If the woman was doing this on the street in broad daylight, who knows how she treated the two little kids behind closed doors?

As we drove by, the woman started screaming at her husband, who had a crying child in each arm.

"What are you doing!?" She ran up to him, waving her arms as if to hit him. "I hate you! I HATE YOU! I wish you would die!"

I stopped the car and watched from across the street. When confronted by this kind of scene, just being present as a witness will often stop the behavior. The woman, losing it completely, was screaming at her husband and children.

"See what I mean by his whining?!" she screamed at the man, who was holding his cowering children. "And now you do this!"

The man said something I couldn't hear and turned his

back on her, walking down the street. The woman went back to the SUV, still shouting after him.

"I want to leave and you have the keys!" she yelled at his back, the children still crying in his arms. The man ignored her and crossed the street with the children. The woman began to press on the SUV's horn.

"GIVE ME THE KEYS!"

"Hey," I called to the woman. "Take a deep breath. You're out of control. I'm going to call the cops."

"Go for it," she snarled, continuing to press on the horn.

Still the man ignored her. The woman ran after the man again and began berating him.

"This woman is out of control," I said to Roberta. "That's child abuse, what she did. I'm going to call the cops."

"You should," Roberta said.

I pulled out my cell phone and dialed 911. For five minutes the scene continued while I listened, incredibly, to a recording. By that time the woman had chased after her family and turned the corner.

"Glad nobody was getting murdered," I muttered, hanging up the phone.

"It's okay," Roberta said. "We stopped her from hitting her kids."

"Yeah," I said. "That time. Those kids will be affected their whole lives by that kind of rage. It will scar them for life."

We drove to the beach, up beautiful Pacific Coast Highway, in a sober mood. The rage the woman had exhibited was disturbing and colored the day. When we got to the beach, we took a swim, washing the incident out of our system and settling on the blanket.

A mother and her small child, a toddler, walked toward

us on the beach. The little girl, who could barely walk, stopped and examined a piece of seaweed. Her mother squatted with her, picking up the seaweed, talking to her daughter, her hand on her back to steady her.

"This comes from the ocean," the woman said.

The little girl flapped her arms, making the seaweed move. She laughed and moved on to a little rock, picking it up and putting it in her mouth. Her mother gently pulled it out of her mouth and the girl sat down. She picked up a fistful of sand and held it up to her mother before throwing it at the water. Her mother did the same, tossing sand at the water. And so they continued on this way, exploring the beach moment by moment. The mother didn't try to make the girl hurry up, didn't try to control her actions so much as guide them. Her mother constantly murmured in her daughter's ear, teaching and explaining the world with endless patience.

It was beautiful to watch. In the space of a half hour, we had seen two completely opposite ways of relating to children. You couldn't get a better example of environmental conditioning; on the one hand the children were experiencing fear and abuse, and on the other love and guidance. They were being programmed like little computers. Would the little boy who was being hit by his mother be filled with rage in his dealings with women later in life? Would he hurt women to overcome his feelings of powerlessness? Or be afraid to enter a long-term relationship? Through his experience with his mother, love is being defined for him as equaling pain. He might spend his life trying to heal his original wound by choosing to be with somebody who feels familiar. He might try to heal his wound over and over, by choosing to be with another abusive woman, in what Freud called "repetition compulsion." However he chooses to deal with it, this abuse is his conditioning.

Compare this with how the little girl is being taught how to relate to herself, to her loved ones, and to the world at large. She is being loved and supported and taught and nurtured. The fruit of her conditioning will likely be more self-esteem and the inclination to choose situations in which she feels cherished.

And such is the dance of conditioning, an accident of birth to which we are all at mercy. If we are born in one house, we get one kind of conditioning and are inculcated with one set of beliefs. If we are born into another house, then we may end up with the exact opposite. We may fight to the death for our way of life, our beliefs—which are just an accident. So why identify with this conditioning? *Why draw our identity from it?*

Advaita Vedanta, the non-dualistic teachings upon which this book is based, calls these layers of conditioning the *ko shas,* which obscure the light of our True Self. The koshas are like layers of an onion and form a barrier from realizing our true nature of bliss and oneness with the universe. When we can clearly see through the layers of the koshas, we awaken from our conditioning, physical, emotional, and psychological. We see reality clearly, without the lenses of our own experience.

In the West, we might characterize this conditioning as part of the nature/nurture paradigm that makes us humans what we are. "Nurture" comprises the experiences we undergo in life, creating the "voices" in our heads. The abused little boy may grow up with a voice that says "I'm worthless." He might act out, believing those voices and thoughts to be true. The "nature" part is the other 50 percent, namely our genetic and biologic inheritance. For instance, there is a gene called 5-HTT that determines why some people react to stressful events such as death, abuse, or job loss by falling into deep depression or paralyzing anxiety, while others are much less affected by the same events. Which version of the gene you get will determine your behavior. This is the nature part of the equation that formulates our personality.

But what lies underneath this personality is the consciousness that informs and supports everything that is, both the "good" conditioning and the "bad" conditioning. So, if it is all one blast of consciousness, why create separation and disconnection from the parts we don't like? The less identified we are with the small self, the personality, the more we are able to feel connection with all that is—we are not contracted down to me, me, and me. Ironically, we then become liberated and we can really let our personality rip. We become looser and freer because we know that it is not really us; what we really are is the clear and present awareness from which it all arises.

Again, this can only be experienced by dropping one's identification with the small self.

But if it's all a manifestation of consciousness or God or whatever the great mystery is called, how can I feel that one way is better than the other? Where does the meaning of right and wrong come from? Why try to intervene with an enraged mother publicly abusing her children? One of the objections people have to the dharma is that if it's all God, why not accept it all, why bother doing anything? Or why not do anything you want? It's all God, right? So what's the difference?

The answer is that the more you marinate in this awareness, in the sacredness of everything, the more you'll see that the abusive mom and the loving mom are opposite sides of the same coin. One is there to help define the other because love brings up everything unlike itself to be healed. The abusive mom is there because she isn't awake. The loving mom is there to help wake her up. And so consciousness plays endlessly with itself in infinite ways.

The abusive mother conditions her children in the same way she was conditioned. This is how it gets passed on. But labeling her bad or evil prevents us from seeing her as the victim she undoubtedly was. And saying she is evil or bad means that we deny that part of ourselves. We can't intersect with her in a meaningful way because to say she is "other" is to deny her humanity. To deny her humanity means we can do anything to her and we end up denying our own. But, given the same conditioning, we could all be the one hitting our children on the street. In fact, many times we are most brutal to those whom we do "love."

Consciousness comes in all forms, and sometimes it indeed plays rough. Sometimes all you can do is be a witness to this roughness.

The antidote to this is wakefulness. To be awake doesn't mean you do anything you want because "nothing matters," but to become supremely aware because *everything matters*. You are aware of your own pain and every bit of pain that you might be causing. You are not running over people, you have empathy and compassion in this awareness. So when a person has an unrequited crush on you, you don't exploit them sexually or mine them for expensive dinners; you treat them gently and with honesty.

Part of waking up is accepting that there are infinite

shades between the light and the dark. Waking up is being able to see them and accept them as parts of ourselves and as integral to everything that is. Being successful in a relationship is to know that light and dark exist in all of us.

So, in the face of extreme bits of consciousness and behavior, you are fine. Simply relax. Know that the awareness at the core of the layers of experience and conditioning for all beings can never be touched, stained, or destroyed.

Your body is a wave on the ocean, but it is not the ocean.

Thoughts are the waves on the ocean, but they are not the ocean.

Experience is the waves on the ocean, but it is not the ocean.

Conditioning is the waves on the ocean, but it is not the ocean.

So don't identify with any of these things, because you are the ocean.

Untouched. Free. Beautiful.

So dance alone and love not just your small self.

Feel the love of being connected to the large Self, all that is.

Even if it plays rough.

*Especially* if it plays rough.

# SELF-INQUIRY

## What Do You Want?

You live in illusion and the appearance of things.
When you understand this, you will see that you are
nothing. And being nothing, you are everything.

KALU RINPOCHE

"I don't know about her . . . she's seems fine, but she doesn't seem like she'd be the type of person who would like to go camping," my friend Charlie said.

Charlie was telling me about a woman he'd just started dating. He was a person who had quite a clear picture of the woman he wanted: petite, natural, spiritual, healthy, and into the outdoors. Carol, the woman in question, is a former model and takes her spiritual life quite seriously. When they met, Charlie had just asked out Suzanne, an acquaintance of Carol's, and they all ended up at a party together. Charlie had asked both women out, but as yet hadn't gone on a date with either of them. By the end of that evening, after a long conversation with both, Charlie was much more interested in Carol than in Suzanne.

The next day, Carol, who had picked up on Suzanne's interest in Charlie, asked Charlie about it in an honest and forthright manner.

"What's your relationship with Suzanne?" Carol asked. "I sensed some energy between the two of you. Are you dating?"

Charlie told her the truth, that he had just met her in the same week as Carol and that the second time he had seen her was that night. Charlie told Carol that he was more interested in pursuing his connection with her than with Suzanne, and that he wasn't going to ask Suzanne out again. And that was the end of the conversation.

This may seem simple, but it is a key indicator of how Carol will handle difficult or sticky issues in the future. Good communication is at the core of a good relationship. Charlie's old girlfriend Janie, who was so possessive she was literally jealous of the love Charlie showed his dog, would have gone ballistic and created a scene. Or set out to make him jealous, especially at the start of dating. Carol was simple, direct, and honest.

"All this sounds really good, so much better than women who can't deal with your affection for your dog," I observed.

"Yeah . . . I don't know . . . But Carol doesn't like to camp."

"Charlie, when was the last time you went camping?" I asked.

"Last summer." It was now February.

"So . . . you go camping once or twice a year?" I asked Charlie, who nodded. "And you're going to make this a deal-breaker, this idea you have about going out with a woman who loves to camp, when you only go once or twice a year yourself? And the ability to communicate, something that actually makes for a good relationship in the day-to-day, something she's already demonstrated, what about that? And not a week later, but right in real time, without any kind of emotional charge. You would toss that aside for . . . camping?"

Charlie shrugged helplessly.

"May I remind you that Janie *loved* to camp. Need I say more?"

Charlie looked at me, shaking his head. "I guess I sound kind of crazy."

Yes. But we all sound crazy at some point or another. We are told to make a list of the qualities we want a prospective mate to have. This sounds great in theory, clarifying what we want a mate to be like, eliminating the qualities that we don't want. But while it can be useful to hold a vision of the qualities we desire, it can also be quite limiting.

*If we have a strict idea of what the other person should look like, then we might miss out on the living and breathing person right in front of us.*

It's pretty rare that people find the perfect person they've been dreaming of their entire life. Finding a partner is about seeing the other person for their innate qualities and not for how they match up against your checklist, which, after all, could be very limited. Perhaps you haven't even imagined who it is that might be right for you. Or perhaps you're too focused on irrelevant qualities like a mutual interest in camping. Either way, you end up approaching the world with expectations, which limits your ability to see reality. When you have expectations, you are seeing the world through the goggles of those expectations. You cannot be present with what is.

Again, one of the main benefits of the dharma, and why I personally think it should be taught in schools, is that it helps us to see reality as it is, rather than as we want it to be. This is true whether on the personal level, as in seeing a lover clearly, or on the level of international relations, as in the situation in Iraq. Secretary of Defense Donald Rumsfeld, before the war, went on and on about the need to see the world clearly, not to have a "failure of expectation," but ultimately he fell into that very trap in Iraq. He was committed to the ideology of "transformation" in the military, insisting on a fraction of the troops his generals said would be needed to secure the country after the war. He was so enamored with the *idea* of a light, fast military, that he ignored all the warning signs. We all see the result of his stubborn shortsightedness now.

This same dynamic is at play interpersonally: How often do we insist on an ideology of transformation with our lovers? How often do we ignore all sorts of signs because a person fits our fixed idea of what we want, and so we then see only what we want to see in that person?

Some people may argue that there is no objective reality; they might say that we are all at the mercy of our own subjective filters. This is only partially true. It's been my experience that there is a spectrum of wakefulness. On the one hand there are fully enlightened people, like the Buddha. On the other, there are people who are deep in the quagmire of their own story, what we call narcissism. But there is an objective reality, and the more awake we are, the closer we get to seeing it.

So rather than making a list of the qualities you want,

like "handsome" or "smart" or "sexy" or "loves to travel," try to think in terms of values. Does the person you are considering share the same values you do? Because they could be handsome, smart, sexy, and a real globe-trotter, but if they don't share your values, that is, *what you find valuable,* then you will have a very long slog. I know a woman who had created a list describing the man of her dreams, including "spiritual," "well-traveled," and "creative." And the man she married is all these things, but he's also a workaholic, impatient, unable to relax, not comfortable with intimacy, and doesn't want to have children. They have been together for three years and haven't had a moment's peace.

The other aspect of creating a list is that you have to subscribe to the New Age belief that you can "manifest your reality"—that by making a list and checking it twice, you can then draw that person to you in some way. But that is a belief system that can cause a great deal of disappointment and self-recrimination. The "create your own reality" school of spirituality gets it half right. If you work on becoming awake, kind, and compassionate, then you will naturally draw similar people into your orbit. If you meet the world with negativity or violence, then you will draw similar people and experiences. This is simply a truism and a way we create our social reality.

But to sit down and make a list and then envision a man or a woman appearing as a result of that visualization, that is ridiculous—subscribing to a belief system that isn't backed up by any empirical fact. Better to wake up so you can see reality clearly and see the people who show up in your life as they really are. In this way you can see them clearly and compassionately. This will also help you make good decisions in choosing a partner.

Making lists, as Charlie did, can lead to a kind of narrowness of vision that might eliminate the right person. The bottom line is that reality is just fine the way it is; it doesn't need to change for you to be happy. In fact, one way to ensure you won't be happy is to make changing reality your lifelong mission. A day or two after our original conversation, Charlie called me again.

"She's got fake breasts."

"Who's got fake breasts?"

"Carol. I touched them. I'm not sure what I feel about that. They feel . . . hard. What do you think that means about a person, that they would get fake breasts? I'm the most natural person in the world and I'm dating a girl who has fake breasts!"

Charlie was again telling himself a story about the "type" of girl he should be going out with. I asked him what really bothered him about the breast implants. Was it how they looked? No. Was it how they felt? Not really, because he had learned to work around their hardness. He acknowledged that they actually looked fine, not overdone or unnatural. It was more the *idea* of them that bothered him—what it said about her as a person, that she was trying to fix herself from the outside in, trying to feel good based on something as superficial as looks.

With plastic surgery becoming more and more common, these are legitimate questions to be asking. Was Carol just another victim of a superficial way of dealing with insecurity, plastering on external solutions rather than taking the more difficult road of self-examination and self-acceptance? Or was she a person who had done a lot of work on herself and still felt she wanted to have the procedure?

When we looked at it, breaking it down, Charlie acknowledged that Carol was, by all measurements, a person with a strong commitment to personal growth. And a person with maturity and impeccable integrity. Charlie enjoyed her company and they actually had fun together.

"But maybe we should have a discussion about her breasts," Charlie said.

"Maybe you should just concentrate on accepting her as she is, rather than as you think she should be," I said. "Believe me, you'll both be much happier. Camping, breasts, whatever—these aren't important."

Charlie nodded. "You're right. This is all in my head."

As far as I know, he never brought the issue up with Carol. They are still together today.

Waking up means setting aside your prejudices, your ideas of what should be, and even your ideas about what you think you want. That way you are in the moment, and by being in the moment you can find yourself pleasantly surprised. You get to see people clearly, without the filters of projection.

Then who knows what can happen, because you're not limiting your view of what is possible.

# EXPERIENCE

## Getting It "Wrong" to Get It Right

*If you love the sacred and despise the ordinary,
you are still bobbing in the ocean of delusion.*

LIN-CHI

As a fellow traveler on this path called life, I have made every mistake in love that there is to make. And I wouldn't change them, no matter how painful, because they were integral to my personal growth. Every hole we fall into teaches us something. Even the worst experiences can be important catalysts for growth.

So, what is the story you are telling yourself about the relationships you've had? Are you telling yourself that you have *failed*? That the relationships you've had are *failures*?

To this I would say *there is no such thing as a failed relationship*. Every relationship you have becomes an integral part of who you are. Every relationship that you started was a mirror of your interior landscape. It was a mirror of where you were at that moment. If you are uncertain how you are doing in your life and how you feel about yourself, take a close look at the people you are attracting. They will perfectly reflect where you are in your spiritual journey. They will show you your conditioning, loud and clear. Because in the realm of personal relationships, we create our own reality by whom we choose.

I have a friend right now who's a screenwriter and is flat broke. He's single. He's at the end of his rope in Hollywood and deeply doubts that he can make a living at his chosen profession. When I asked him if he was dating anybody, he said, wisely, that he wouldn't want to date the woman he would choose when he was in such a depressed and desperate state. In this way, he put his finger on what I call the mirroring principle. The people with whom we choose to be in a relationship mirror exactly how we feel about ourselves and what we think we deserve.

While it helps not to be in the basement of yourself, it doesn't mean you have to be perfect in order to be in a relationship, for whoever you choose to be with will help you grow, intentionally or unintentionally. In fact, while there is "perfection" in solitude, there is usually much more opportunity for growth in a relationship; it's easy to cruise along when you're single. But if you learn the lessons of each relationship, if you grow and transform yourself in this journey called life, how can your connections with the people you share it with be called a "failure"? They were perfect in that moment of your life, to learn the lessons that you needed.

Let's face it—we all choose our lovers based on a strange cocktail of need, desire, conditioning, and projection. We don't know *what we're doing* when we smile and say hi to the next love of our life. We are completely blind to *what is,* because we are only seeing *what we want to see.* We're not awake, we're in a dream, unconsciously choosing our partners based on subterranean urges that we aren't even aware of, never mind understand.

You know the old joke about the masochist and the sadist who go to a large party with two hundred people in it? Within minutes they're talking to each other. Well, we're all a little bit like that. Call it lust, call it love, call it conditioning, but many times you can call it: Ka-chung! Interlocking dysfunction.

So there you are, in a relationship, learning about your partner and, one hopes, learning about yourself. Because that's what a relationship is there for. It's not just to have fun. It's not just for great sex, groovy weekend trips, and the pride of having somebody desirable on your arm. It's not even there to end up in marriage and happily-ever-after.

Because while all of that might happen—it is important and fun and even sometimes about celebration and pleasure—it will most certainly fade. In fact, the difference between pleasure and happiness is that pleasure is fleeting. We chase pleasure, and while we have it we are content. But when we lose it we are forlorn. Happiness is different. Happiness is your natural state and birthright. Happiness is underneath all of the other conditioning, and the source of the happiness is not mere pleasure. The source of that happiness is the realization that you are Love and you are connected to all that is.

But at the end of the day, every relationship will end. If it ends before death because of separation or divorce, does that mean it is a failure? No. Only if you don't learn from it can it be considered a mistake. Because if you don't learn from your current relationship, you will just go ahead and repeat the same exact dynamic with somebody else. It will be a case of different face, same person.

So, when a relationship ends, don't look at it as failure. Look at your lover as your partner in growth, both spiritual and psychological—like a tennis player who plays with you for the joy of the game, but also to make you a better player.

You are in your relationship for your own spiritual growth. It won't always be fun, and sometimes the spiritual lesson you may need to learn is to walk away, but nonetheless, it is about your growth.

Do you still feel that a relationship that ends is a failed relationship?

Does the fact that you might be single as you read these words make you a failure? Does it make you a loser? Are you telling yourself a real whopper, like "I'm a borderline psychopath incapable of sustaining any long-term relationships"? What other stories are you telling yourself?

The point is that every relationship, no matter how screwed up and painful, was there for you to get to where you are now, operating at a higher plane of awareness (if you've truly learned from your relationships).

I have had a lot of relationships, some as long as five years, others as short as five months. Each one has been a bit of getting it wrong to finally get it right. Each one has shown me where I am and has prepared me for the next.

So be gentle with yourself. Be forgiving of all the crazy choices you have made.

We all do it all the time. And it's not what we have done,

but how we learn and grow from what we have done that counts.

And in the dharma, often it's not what we do or what situations we find ourselves in that is important. It's the stories we tell ourselves afterwards that add the unnecessary suffering or self-blame. Staying stuck in the past, telling yourself any story about the relationship that is over, is a prescription for suffering.

All your relationship experience is in the past.

The story you tell yourself about it is not you.

In this moment, you are free. And it is only in this moment that you can possibly be awake to the possibilities that surround you.

Right now.

# SOUL MATES

## What Does It Even Mean?

*The eyes are windows of the soul.*

WILLIAM SHAKESPEARE

"He's my soul mate," my friend Janice sighed dreamily. "I have finally found the *one,* the one person I've been waiting my whole life for."

We were sitting in a restaurant, and her new boyfriend was on the way. Janice is thirty-five, smart, and pretty—a serial monogamist whom I've known for a decade.

"I'm so happy for you," I said. "When did you meet him? When did all this start? I mean, I've only been out of town for a couple of weeks."

"That's all it takes with the right one," Janice said. "I knew the minute I saw him."

"Wow," I said, wanting to be supportive. "That's amazing."

David came in, and we stood up from the table. Janice and David rushed into each other's arms for a lingering hug and a kiss.

"Hi, I'm David." He disengaged for a moment to shake my hand. He was tall, with a quick smile and eyes that immediately slid sideways back to Janice. We had dinner, and during the whole time they snuggled up to each other, never breaking contact—always touching each other's arms and glancing at one another. At one point David actually switched his fork to his left hand so he could sit closer to her in the booth, putting his arm around her. In fact, he seemed more adoring of her than she did of him.

Three weeks later, Janice broke up with David, stating that he was too needy. Two weeks after that, he was stalking her. She finally had to get a restraining order against him, which, luckily for her, he obeyed.

After enough time had passed and she could finally laugh about it, we had dinner again.

"So . . . now that your soul mate has been warned off by the police, where does that leave you regarding love?"

"Ha, ha, very funny, Arthur," Janice said, smirking. "I don't know, I guess I'll have to find another soul mate."

"Really?" I said. "Maybe you should forget about the idea of a soul mate."

"Why?" she asked.

"I think that true love is not about anointing somebody as special—it sets a trap of expectation. If they are 'special,' then they must continue to be special instead of who they really are. As soon as they lose their 'specialness,' the gloss of infatuation goes off the relationship and we become dissatisfied. They have disappointed us by being human, with flaws and faults all their own."

"That's crazy," Janice said. "What about preferences? What about liking people because of their personalities?"

"Well, there are personality types that are more compatible. But true love gives love to all who encounter it."

"What a bizarre idea," Janice mused. "Then nobody is special."

"Exactly—everybody is special. It all depends on whether we want to be in an ego-based relationship or whether we want to drop our identification with our ego needs and feel our connection with all that is."

"One is dependent upon other people," Janice said slowly. "The latter is free and infinite."

"Yes," I said. "Exactly right."

I'm more and more convinced that it doesn't matter who you love—it could be anybody. As in many happy arranged marriages, the love actually follows the commitment. This is not to say that there aren't certain personalities that are more compatible with our own; there are, but the intrinsic humanity in each of us is the same. And it is the act of being loving that makes for a successful union. This is contrary to most of our romantic notions in the West of finding our one true love.

We talked for a long time about what she thought had happened between her and David. Who was he to her? Why did she go for him and hand over her complete heart, lock, stock, and both barrels? We covered her projections, the fact that you don't know anybody when you first meet them. We talked about infatuation as the most powerful drug on the planet, stimulating the pleasure centers of the brain in the same way that heroin does. Janice talked extensively about how David was emotionally similar to her own sister, who was also extremely needy.

"Erich Fromm said there's a difference between 'I love you because I need you' and 'I need you because I love you,' " I said. "The first one is dependency, not love. People get it mixed up all the time, myself included."

"I don't get the difference," Janice said, repeating the phrases again.

"If you love somebody because you need them, you're expecting them to fulfill your needs. It puts tremendous pressure on the other person. You might have felt a bit of that with David."

Janice rolled her eyes.

"Just a bit."

"Loving somebody because you need them is also not authentic love. It's a form of codependency. And as soon as they stop fulfilling your needs, watch out!"

"Yeah, they start showing up outside your workplace."

"Right. But if you need somebody because you love them, the love comes first. There isn't the same kind of pressure."

"Yeah, I felt a lot of pressure."

"But what about the pressure you put on him?" I asked.

"What pressure? I just seriously fell for him, until he started wigging out."

"Really? What about the pressure of him being your 'soul mate'? Not to mention the pressure you put on yourself and the relationship."

"I thought he was my one and only soul mate. But I was wrong." Janice started to sound defensive.

"It's not about being right or wrong. It's about expectations. I would just throw out the idea of 'soul mate.' "

"I'm sure he's out there."

"But what does that mean?"

"The one person in the whole world who was meant for

me," Janice said, and then she burst out laughing. "I guess that sounds ridiculous."

"Yeah. Out of the six billion people on the planet, there's only one person with whom you could have a happy life?"

We both started laughing.

"I mean, what if he was Chinese and you never had a chance to meet him? Or what if David was him, but it didn't work out? Are you off to a nunnery for the rest of your life?"

"Not likely." She grinned. "By the way, I've been to China. I could have met him there."

"Yeah, yeah."

We talked about it for quite a while—how on some level we are all waiting around for that one person with whom we have a magical connection, love at first sight, the person with whom we can merge and sink into each other's eyes. But how many times has that happened and it blew up in your face? How many times, after that strange brew of projection and infatuation, have you ended up feeling as if you didn't know the other person at all? They are as blank as a movie screen upon which we run our own movie, telling ourselves the story we want to hear. Until one day, as in that Talking Heads song, we wake up and say, "This is not my beautiful house. This is not my beautiful wife . . ."

True love is different from material love. True love is not about the experience of falling in love or infatuation, which depends upon "love chemicals" that get released in the brain, along with large dollops of projection. As I mentioned earlier, a relationship that begins with our need for the other person's love is doomed to fail unless it matures into spiritual love.

We get so caught up in the story of what is happening that we don't even see what is really happening!

In Janice's case it was the "soul mate" story.

"Okay. I get what you're saying. But what is true love?" Janice asked.

"My experience is that it's not just a feeling. It is an action. Love is a verb. You can't experience walking or eating without actually doing the actions of walking and eating. The same is true for loving."

"So it isn't simply a case of getting lucky enough to run into the one person out of the six billion that's going to do it for you?" Janice cracked up laughing.

"Right," I said, grinning. "Most people, however, treat love as a noun, an object that can be bought, attained, bartered, and lost. It's like an addict to his dealer—we look to other people to be our love supplier."

"Hook me up, baby."

"Right. You might as well face it . . ." Janice joined me in singing the song. "You're addicted to love!"

Once we stopped laughing, I said, "Rather than looking to give love without expectation in return, we are always looking to *get* love. But true love is about *acting in a loving way*. This means not categorizing, pressuring, or having expectations of your lover. It means that by being loving, you tend to the love in the relationship. It's not whimsical, it doesn't appear one week and disappear the next. It is the dharma of loving."

And this is the secret. It doesn't matter what or who you love. It's all the same because true love is an *element*. The more you drop your identification with your own needs and personality, the more you will feel love as a current that runs through everything. You will feel love for everybody.

So forget about finding your soul mate. What pressure! What an abstraction! What a distraction! Love the person who is in front of you right now. Notice how that feels, notice how that creates a sense of connection.

And try to see them clearly. The greatest gift you can give is to see someone clearly, allowing them to be who they are and where they are in the great mystery that is a life unfolding.

# CASUAL SEX

## Oxytocin Alert!

*When we have loved, my love,*
*Panting and pale from love,*
*Then from our cheeks, my love,*
*Scent of the sweat I love:*
*And when our bodies love*
*Now to relax in love*
*After the stress of love,*
*Ever still more I love*
*Our mingled breath of love.*

SANSKRIT VERSE

When you meet somebody, there is immediate attraction. Or not.

It can be as binary as that. And there really isn't anything you need to do to engender chemistry; it's there or it isn't. But understand that no matter how attracted you are, you don't know the other person at all. This may seem obvious, but in the heat of a first greet, sometimes the obvious goes out the window.

And sometimes things can get going a bit faster than we want. I mean, sometimes you're sleeping with somebody before you would agree to share a toothbrush with them!

Why does this happen, and what does it mean? Chemistry is that great mystery that has nothing to do with looks or common background or shared beliefs. It often doesn't have anything to do with whether you even like the other person. Have you ever played the game where you shut your eyes and listened to your brand-new lover? Or pretended your lover was two hundred pounds heavier, and then looked at their behavior, intelligence, and beliefs? Would you still "love" them, or would you be out the door? It's a good litmus test because chemistry is a powerful cocktail that has no interest in your well-being, good or bad. It just wants to jump. A modified version of the old saying might be "Chemistry is as chemistry does."

And so you might be able to fall into bed with somebody very quickly. You might tell yourself that this is just some fun. You might come to a complete understanding with your sexual partner that "this is nothing serious." Or perhaps you are telling yourself that you're not ready for a real relationship, that this fling is just about enjoyment and pleasure. Your partner, whether a man or a woman, might be in complete agreement that what is happening is purely recreational, that you are "friends with benefits." In fact, in suburban America, where oral sex is now common by eighth or ninth grade and "hookups" are as casual as a handshake, you can be seen as weird if you don't partake. To quote a *New York Times* (May 30, 2004) article on the subject:

It's not that teenagers have given up on love alto-
gether. Most of the high-school students I spent time
with said they expect to meet the right person, fall in
love and marry—eventually. It's just that high school,
many insist, isn't the place to worry about that. High
school is about keeping your options open. Relationships are about closing them. As these teenagers see
it, marriage and monogamy will seamlessly replace
their youthful hookup careers sometime in their mid-
to late twenties—or, as one high-school boy from
Rhode Island told me online, when "we turn thirty
and no one hot wants us anymore."

As a person who is past thirty, I can smile at that last
sentence. But what about the commonly held notion "if it
feels good in the moment, do it"? Isn't that what these
teachings are all about? Being in the moment?

But this is a misunderstanding of the teachings. To be
awake means seeing the world clearly and allowing your
own true nature to shine through. And what is that true nature? It's love. And what is the highest form of love? It's
compassion, not exploitation.

If I were in high school and getting oral sex at the drop
of a hat, it might seem pretty good. As a man, I might even
think, darn, I was born too early. But the truth of that situation is that the teenage girls aren't getting oral sex in exchange. They aren't even getting sexual pleasure in return.
They aren't getting experience and knowledge of how to
build a real relationship out of these hookups. What they
are getting is depressed. What they are getting are sexual
diseases—female adolescents aged fifteen to nineteen have

the highest incidence of both gonorrhea and chlamydia, according to the latest CDC figures.

But what about adults? Surely consensual sex with both partners informed of what's going on is okay, right? I mean, what are we supposed to do, live like monks?

I've had plenty of experience with recreational sex, and I make no moral judgments about it. How could I? But what happens when you don't treat making love like *making love,* is you reduce your capacity for intimacy. You reduce your capacity to love. You reduce your sensitivity by forming a relationship based on consumption and objectification. In your push for more stimulation, more meaningless experience, and more pleasure, you diminish your ability to feel. You are chasing pleasure, which always passes, leaving you seeking even more pleasure. You think you are free, but you are actually creating a bondage to the dynamic of sensation-seeking. Trying to fill up a hole in yourself with sex, the same way an alcoholic tries to fill it with booze, can lead to sexual addiction.

The truth is, when you do this, it is like pouring water into a bucket with a hole in it—it can never be filled. And using people in this way perpetuates a kind of violence against them.

Now hold on a minute, you might be saying. Violence?

We are all sensitive creatures—even the most "armored" of us is sensitive, hiding behind that armor to keep from getting hurt again. When you are using another person for sexual gratification, without the heart being engaged, it is a form of objectification and somebody will get hurt— that's just the way things work. And it may well be you. You might develop feelings for a person with whom you are completely incompatible. You might fall in love and the other person might not care about you. Or they might fall in love and you will be left with a person whom you have seduced and then abandoned because for you it was simply casual, but for them it was the world.

There is another aspect to it, especially for men. We think we are living it up the most if we sleep with a lot of partners. The more powerful we are, the more opportunities we have to go from person to person, and we think we are getting something out of it. But actually we are losing something; what actually happens is that we reduce our capacity for intimacy. By going wide and shallow, we become inured to the pleasures of diving deep with one person. Eventually we are burnt out, overstimulated, shallow, and in need of a psychic rehabilitation just to learn how to feel something again.

Again, I want to stress that this is not to say we shouldn't honor attraction and chemistry. It is what separates lovers from friends; partners to whom we're not initially attracted have a tendency to fade. So don't be overly spiritual about this—don't label chemistry as "not spiritual." While lust isn't love, desire is a legitimate ingredient for a good partnership.

But the farther down the path of wakefulness you travel, the less you will be able to enter these arenas without knowing the potency of the elements with which you play. You discover the thrill of flinging open the doors of your heart with another human being and saying, "I'm committed, you're it!" You free-fall into the depths of your own heart and discover that sex is much more intense, rewarding, and fulfilling when you take the risk of emotional involvement.

Giving love is the way in which we approach divine love, a love that isn't outside of us, isn't dependent on other people or even an external deity. Divine love is a simple acknowledgment of this reality: it is *all* love. Even so-called evil is a form of love, just one that is deeply obscured or perverted by pain. As Marianne Williamson said, "It's all love or a cry for help."

So try to be careful rather than careless. Sexual relationships are like Roach Motels, easy to enter and very difficult to exit, for the simple reason that when you're embarking on what you think is a casual sexual relationship, your body's hormones are busily bonding with your partner, whether you want to or not. On a purely biological level, the hormone oxytocin, which rises as a result of human touch, kicks in.

Oxytocin makes us feel good about the person who causes the hormone to be released, and it causes a deep bonding between the two people. Nursing a baby produces oxytocin in both mother and child, and this is a major part of what initially bonds the mother and her baby. Even thinking of someone we love can stimulate this hormone; when women in good marriages were asked to think about their husbands, the level of oxytocin in their blood quickly rose.

Oxytocin plays a significant role in our sexuality. Higher levels of oxytocin result in greater sexual receptivity, and because oxytocin increases testosterone production (which is responsible for sex drive in both men and women), sex drive can also increase. And while oxytocin can move us toward sex, sex increases production of oxytocin: nipple stimulation, genital stimulation, and intercourse all raise the levels of oxytocin in men and women. Orgasm causes levels to spike even higher, three to five times normal, creating the afterglow closeness that is experienced following lovemaking. The fact that sex increases oxytocin levels can be helpful for women who complain they "never feel like sex." When you have sex, even when you don't have a drive to do so, it will actually affect you in ways that will result in a greater sex drive. This also explains, at least in part, why many people find that the more sex they have, the more they want, and the less sex they have, the less they want.

But this bonding phenomenon doesn't only have to do with sex. Touch is vital to humans, and most of us don't get nearly enough of it. Babies deprived of touch don't develop normally because certain connections in the brain actually disappear. Orphans who receive very little touch often die as a result, and those who survive can experience permanent physical and mental retardation. Kids who don't get enough touch grow up to become aggressive and antisocial adults. Older adults who don't get enough touch also suffer, becoming senile sooner, and dying earlier. We're all affected by touch, and it's not "all in the mind"; rather, it's the result of complex hormonal responses that actually change our bodies and brains.

So touch and be touched. But the desire for touch can be fulfilled in many ways; through a hug from a friend or a massage, physical connection is available everywhere. It doesn't have to be sexualized. In fact, many times people looking for intimacy or comfort will resort to sex in order to get it.

But understand that when you take it to the most physically intimate act possible between two human beings, it will be hard to keep things casual. The heart will become engaged, maybe not right away, but within three or four couplings. Once you understand that this bonding happens, you must, if awake, treat it with responsibility. Love means treating the other person with respect and kindness, but it also means *taking care:* taking care of the other person's emotional and spiritual well-being instead of fulfilling your own needs; taking care of their hearts. I am speaking particularly to men here, because a woman's heart will become engaged, gentlemen. It is human nature.

And if the heart doesn't get involved, then the essential part of you is being cut off from the act. You are going numb in the very area that the sex is supposed to be expressing. Sex without love is ultimately empty. Moments after orgasm, you wish the other person would simply disappear. Haven't we all been there, wishing there was a magic button? I have. For a long time I tried to do it, but no matter how intense the sex was, something was missing. And when I met somebody and fell in love and really *made love with them,* there was a tremendous relief; there was a release in the heart.

When engaging sex with love, you are committed to putting the most vulnerable part of yourself in the hands of another. You become willing to risk getting your heart broken, for, in the end, it's a heartbreaking world. Out of this risk comes a deepened ability to love. We are on the planet to give and receive love. We then take the love we feel for another person and use it as a portal into a love and connection to all that is. The only alternative is to contract, shut down, and numb out. For in all love there is the reality of loss: loss of the idea, loss of romance, loss of physical attraction, and eventually the actual loss of the person.

But we don't have to be dead people walking. We don't have to anticipate the loss by killing off a part of our heart in order not to feel pain. We don't have to numb out by treating sex as purely recreational.

This has nothing to do with guilt about sex as passed on by dualistic religions, which try to separate our bodies from our spirit. Those religions were created when women were nothing more than chattel, something to be bartered or traded and whose value was determined by their virginity. The sacred feminine has been distorted by religion and the church. Instead of a revered union of the two halves of the human spirit—male and female—through which both could find spiritual wholeness and communion with God, sex is viewed as a sin, a perversion, and something to be resisted except in marriage for the purpose of procreation. This consolidated the church's self-proclaimed status as the sole conduit to God. By demonizing sex and recasting it as a disgusting and sinful act, the church eliminated mankind's early pagan use of sex to commune directly with God. Our ancient heritage and our physical urges tell us sex is natural—a cherished route to spiritual fulfillment—and yet modern religion teaches us to fear our sexual desire as the hand of the devil. This horrible distortion, the cause of so much pain and suffering by women at the hands of male patriarchy, is not the reason to avoid casual sex. My thoughts on sex have nothing to do with "morality," an externally imposed set of rules that must be followed. But they have everything to do with the organic laws of love. An apple falls from a tree, not because of external rules, but because of the laws of physics; it is simply the way the world works. In the nondualistic teachings, sex is a beautiful thing. But if it is disconnected from love, it often becomes a painful and contracted experience. This is just the way love works.

But don't take my word for it. Just notice the difference

when you are with somebody with just your body versus being with somebody when your heart is engaged. Feel what it's like not to hold your heart back.

As the poet James Russell Lowell said, "God's angels come to us disguised."

Sex is simply the most powerful way to deepen our expression of love and commune with the infinite face of God.

# GAY OR STRAIGHT OR BI

## Love Is Love

*The best lack all conviction, while the worst*
*Are full of passionate intensity.*

—WILLIAM BUTLER YEATS, "THE SECOND COMING"

As I write this, the Massachusetts Supreme Court has just legalized same-sex marriage, much to the chagrin of many. By the time you read this, it may or may not have been blocked by various legislative procedures.

There has been a massive outcry about this legislation, reminiscent of the furor in the late 1950s over interracial couples, who were greeted with similar derision and hostility, if not actual arrest and prosecution.

How do gay couples express deeper commitment in an environment of homophobia and legal blocks to marriage? What do you do in a society where people like Jerry Falwell are still calling homosexuality an abomination, and where the majority of Americans don't support marriage, the ultimate commitment between any two people, for same-sex couples?

One thing to keep in mind is that no matter what happens with this one piece of legislation, the tide is turning and it is only a matter of time before the love expressed between any two people will be accorded the privileges and protections of marriage. It is inevitable. Even though we may have been conditioned to be homophobic from our high school playground or our own parents' belief systems, most of us don't adhere to extreme forms of prejudice and intolerance. We intuitively understand that a live-and-let-live philosophy is the only one that makes any sense. But we have all, to one degree or another, been conditioned.

And so we have the fresh debate on whether gay couples should be allowed to marry. Ultimately it doesn't matter what we think, because *love cannot be stopped*. Like life itself, love cannot be throttled; it will always find a way to grow, like a flower pushing itself up through a crack in the pavement. No matter what the conditioned oppression, no matter what man-made religious "values" are ascribed, no matter what the bigotry, love will always triumph, for, in the long run, that is what love does.

Often gay people have to put up with nonacceptance from family—their own, their partner's, or both. Difficult families, no matter what your sexual orientation, are a part of everyone's dating experience.

I have a friend named Rob who is gay. While attractive, he had spent many years trying to find somebody with whom to have a relationship, and was constantly complaining about the men in Los Angeles.

"It's all about the body," Rob used to say. "Everybody's got this 'gym-boy' mentality. Spend two hours a day getting all buffed, go to the tanning salon to get tanned, get every last hair lasered off. It's impossible to find somebody who's normal and capable of having a conversation."

"Pretty superficial," I said.

"It's beyond superficial, it's pathological."

Years went by and Rob stayed single; I used to tease him that he was gay in name only. In practice, he was a monk. Finally Rob met somebody. Tim was an architect from the East Coast. He was cool, funny, and smart and he never went to the gym. They started to get serious. After a year, they were talking about buying a house together. Then one day Rob called me.

"My parents met Tim and they hated him," he said without preamble, obviously upset.

"What?" I said. "What's not to like? He's a great guy."

"They said . . . they said they just didn't trust him."

"Did anything happen?"

"No, we all went out to dinner and when the check came, Tim was in the bathroom. I went to pick up the bill, but my dad grabbed it. Later my dad said it was a cheesy move to go to the bathroom when the check came." Rob was distraught. "Little things like that. Now they are dead set against us moving in together."

"Do you think it's hard for them?" I said. "I mean, up to now, you've been only theoretically gay. Now here's this guy and he wants to move in with you. It's become a little more real."

"Maybe. But I thought we'd been through all that when I came out."

"Yeah, but you know how it is. There are different layers of acceptance."

"But what am I going to do? They're just adamant. They don't even want him in the house for their big Christmas party."

Though Rob's parents were apparently showing a form of homophobia, this is a situation that comes up in all sorts of relationships, both gay and straight.

How do you cope when your family and friends don't like your partner?

This is an incredibly tricky thing to deal with, because you don't want to alienate your loved ones, but you don't want to insult or devalue your connection with your new lover, either. A close friend of mine confessed one day that he just didn't get his brother's relationship with his live-in girlfriend. He just didn't understand the attraction.

"She's just so boring," he said.

"But, listen, she is fulfilling your brother in some emotional way that you are not experiencing," I said. "You know how hard it is to find anybody to be with, so be supportive and try not to judge it."

"But I don't like her," my friend said.

"You don't have to like her."

Love in all its forms needs to be supported. You don't have to understand the attraction, you don't even have to like the person. But what you must do is respect the commitment two people are trying to make with each other, even people who are always bickering. You don't see the part of the relationship that they experience: the intimacy, the fun, and the intensity. Even under the best of circumstances it is a struggle to overcome fear and to love, so be supportive of healthy relationships when you encounter them.

How do you handle situations in which friends or relatives are unsupportive? Deal with them directly. On some level, family and friends are trying to control your experience of the world. It might be out of malice, prejudice, or even genuine concern. But whatever the reason, it is unacceptable. We all must be free to make our own mistakes. And we must allow others theirs.

The first step to take with somebody who is not respecting your choice is to make it known to them how unacceptable it is; ultimately, people will only respect your relationship to the extent that you respect, fight for, and cherish it. You must make it clear that this is the person you are choosing to be with, and that you would like the support of family and friends, *but the relationship is going forward regardless.*

Often this requires playing a kind of hardball. When Rob confronted his parents, he said that if they were not willing to accept the man in his life, then in a very fundamental way they were not accepting him. Then he told them that he wouldn't be coming home for Christmas that year, but would instead be traveling with Tim.

"Wow," I said to Rob, when he told me the story. "What did they say?"

"They totally freaked out. But I think they got how serious I was." Rob said. "And in a weird way it clarified my feelings for Tim. It will all work out."

And it did. When Rob's family had their big Easter party, Tim was invited, and Rob and Tim are still together today. Eventually the family came around. Gays have to face many more challenges than straight couples do, but times are changing, and with more acts of courage and clarity, they will continue to change, one family at a time.

We are all on the frontlines of our own conditioning, attempting to push it back, attempting to expand our awareness in order to become more gracious, more tolerant, and more loving. That is our journey on the planet, both individually and collectively. And it will be supported by love itself. Love of our gay brothers or sons or daughters.

So notice when you dislike a person. Usually this has to do with our own unprocessed shadow—we despise in other people what we despise in ourselves. But the truth will fight like a drowning hyena to come to the surface, and eventually our shadow will have to be dealt with, either with ourselves or in our relationships with our loved ones.

It is how we evolve, both individually and as a society. It is against love not to allow the plaintiff in the Massachusetts case resulting in the same-sex-marriage legislation, when her partner was in a hospital giving birth, into the neonatal intensive care unit. It is against love not to allow a man to be with his partner of twenty years as he died of AIDS, because he wasn't a "family" member. It is against love not to go to your best friend's wedding because you don't like your friend's prospective spouse. It is against love to skip your son's or daughter's wedding because they chose somebody out of your religion.

In all cases, it is important to trust love. Both as individuals and as a society, we must trust that the love we feel and the love we witness in others is a life-affirming force that will be supported as long as we have the courage to support it. There is no way that the urge to love can be crushed or curtailed. Love will always find a way to express itself.

# GOT KIDS?

## The New Family

There is no remedy for love but to love more.

HENRY DAVID THOREAU

A close friend of mine had a beautiful baby girl after being impregnated by a man she hardly knew. She had had one abortion before that and was devastated by it, so she decided to go ahead and have the baby, even though the father made it quite clear he wasn't interested in raising the child. She has since married and is pregnant with her second child, living the nuclear family dream, albeit with a twist. As a successful music video director, she is the major breadwinner in the family.

When I told my grandmother about my friend's first pregnancy, she reacted with disapproval.

"Having a baby alone is just wrong," she said. "A baby needs both a mother and a father. That's the way it was meant to be."

I knew this was all tied to a view that men and women shouldn't even be having sex before marriage, so I didn't engage her.

"The high rate of divorce, people having bastard kids right and left . . . it's the end of morality," she huffed. Then she pointed her finger at me. "And you should keep your pants on more before you find yourself in the same exact position!"

I laughed.

"I know, I know. I should be a forty-year-old virgin. I'll try harder, Grandmom."

"Yeah." She grinned at me, knowing I was needling her. "Sure you will."

I had my own concerns about my friend, and I struggled with them. I was worried that she wouldn't be able to handle it all alone, even though she is a successful and creative director. I wasn't certain that she understood how much her life was going to change.

But the fact is that only 10 percent of families in the United States fit the so-called typical or traditional family image of mother at home, father at work, first marriage, children of that marriage. And serious questions have been raised about whether that family ever existed in significant numbers in the first place. And whether, when it did exist, it was the ideal that people think it was.

Two recent books, *The Way We Never Were,* by Stephanie Coontz, and *The Politics of Parenthood,* by Mary Frances Berry, provide abundant evidence derived from historical records, census data, and research studies to document their conclusion that it never was the norm. Neither the Victorian family in *Life with Father,* that extended family we like to think about so nostalgically, nor the 1950s *Leave It to Beaver* family was ever the norm, and such families were certainly not without problems when they did exist. Coontz and Berry demonstrate convincingly that our visions of the past, both of family and of American society in general, are largely fiction, that many of the problems we think are new or unique or worse than they have ever been are actually the same or even less serious than in the past.

In Victorian times there was the authoritarian but presumably well-meaning father. Women didn't have the vote. Women and children were considered property by a patriarchal society. Middle-class and wealthy families were dependent upon the work of low-income servants, including mothers who took care of other people's children while their own children often had to be neglected.

The Industrial Revolution brought twelve-to-sixteen-hour days for many working mothers and fathers, sweatshop conditions in factories, child labor, and children left alone at home or on the streets. The post–World War II suburban nuclear family, living in ranch-style houses, had a public image that was often very different from what was really happening behind closed doors. Those households had lonely and depressed moms, stressed commuter dads, drugs, alcohol, and adultery, all of which resulted in the highest divorce rate we've ever known. The women who worked to help their war-veteran husbands go to college and then stayed home to raise the children, often found themselves divorced and replaced by younger women who were the colleagues of their husbands out in the working world. Economically, there was a better life for some families, but not for all. There was discrimination against racial and ethnic groups—violence, intimidation, unequal opportunity, and unemployment. The TV image and the fond recollections don't show reality as it really was.

Poverty in large numbers of families with children is also not unique to our time, and poverty among women and children has always been extensive and disproportionate.

The truth is that families now come in all shapes and sizes. There are gay families raising children, single mothers and fathers, and communal living arrangements. There are families without marriage, and mixed families with children from multiple marriages.

So, what is the best definition of family?

I would say any group of people bound by love.

We don't want to live in a sentimental world, wishing for a reality that never was. Nor do we want to rant against the world as it is. Remember, waking up is a matter of seeing the world and *what is,* not what we want it to be. There are more and more different versions and visions of family. The more we can accept and tolerate those visions, the more we can see them as an expansion of love in our world.

The only alternative is to be shaking our heads and clucking our tongues at the world. The truth is that children always embody an affirmation of life and love. And marriage is an affirmation of commitment to each other and those children. So don't encourage people to get married for moralistic reasons. Encourage it as a commitment to love and as a way to legally protect the children who are bringing that life and love into the world.

And when you are dating somebody with children, understand that they are the top priority in your partner's life. (Think about it—would you want to be with somebody who didn't make their children a priority?) And in most cases the children, except where there is a death in the family, already have a mother or father. So you don't have to rush to fill that role. Let things develop naturally. Be friendly but not pushy, because kids may react extremely negatively to anybody they see as an interloper. They may be jealous of any time that their mother or father is spending with the new person in their life. And they can smell a fake a mile away.

The only thing to do in the case of dating a person with children is to have great patience. If the child's world has been turned upside down by a divorce, remember they are hurting, even if their pain is coming out as anger. Remember, you are the adult; you are the one who is mature and evolved. They are quite literally still evolving, adjusting to a situation that may take them years. So take things slowly.

And if you are the parent just beginning to date, be sensitive to your child's feelings. Depending upon the age of the child, don't bring every person you date around the house and make a big deal about it. If you're not even sure you'll ever see the person again, why subject your child to them? And when you do finally introduce them, if they are young, reassure them that this doesn't mean anything will change with their father or mother.

Whether you are the parent or the person dating the parent, keep in mind that all things are constantly changing. And children are an especially good reminder of this— what might be a huge deal today may well be forgotten tomorrow. But make no mistake that in the moment, children are usually more awake than adults. They will laugh and cry and scream and shout and be in the moment with you. They will also let you know exactly what is going on with them. So flexibility is key.

I have a friend who is dating a woman whose nine-year-old boy initially *hated* him. The child would throw tantrums, be insulting, and ignore him for long periods of time. Instead of imagining that it should be any other way, he accepted the boy unconditionally, treating him with unfailing respect and kindness. Eventually the boy came around. Children know when somebody really cares, so be really caring. Your kindness will thaw them out.

As for my old friend who is pregnant with her second child, her husband now wants to adopt the two-year-old running around underfoot. She is thrilled. Her home is warm and filled with love and life.

She created a new family based on love, not doctrine.

# GOSSIP

## Find a Better Way to Bond

Rumor travels faster,
but it don't stay put as long as truth.

WILL ROGERS

Is there anything better than a tidbit of juicy gossip? The titillation, the judgment, and the conspiratorial closeness it breeds can be very intoxicating. It can also become so habitual that it's addictive, and can create so much pain that it's difficult to undo.

Gossip is a hard thing to give up, because it supplies so many needs: the need to know what is going on with people and the need to understand human nature. It also satisfies the desire to be close to the person with whom you're gossiping. People gather around a piece of gossip as if it were a cozy campfire. It makes you seem closer to the people with whom you gossip, but it's a false currency. Like doing cocaine at five in the morning with a bunch of strangers, the

camaraderie lasts only as long as the drugs. And the hang-
over of judgment is usually right on the heels of gossip.

As a writer, a dharma teacher, and a student of human
nature, I like to discuss people and what motivates them. I
like to think that I can understand them. And what's the
harm in that? Well, on the surface, nothing. I try to figure
out what makes people tick and discuss this with a couple
of friends who have similar interests in the interior lives
of their fellow humans. Most of us are writers, constantly
looking at character and motivation in our work. And sometimes I can get to a point of rueful understanding, seeing
it all with amused benevolence. But often it just ends up
with a sense of separation and judgment. It is also reduc-
tive, for how much about another human being can you
really know?

I've tried to change my ways from talking about people
in this way. It's hard, but I've come to realize that you can
never really know what another person is going through.
Nor can you know what both sides of a story are. And, finally, most things we gossip about are things we have actually done ourselves.

Even when you think you are doing some good, say,
warning somebody of another person's behavior, it can get
very sticky.

I can remember a time when a guy named Paul began
dating Suzanne, a friend of mine. Paul came on very strong
and then, according to her, turned on a dime and disappeared. She was crushed. It took her a while to get over
it. A year later, Alicia, a woman I had been seeing casually
for a couple of months, ended it abruptly and began dating
Paul. Alicia and I stayed friends, and she went on and on
about Paul. I told Alicia what had happened between Paul

and Suzanne, how Paul had come on strong and suddenly split, telling her to be careful and to take things slowly.

Little did I know that Alicia was going to tell Paul what I was saying about him. This was seven years ago and we've all grown up since then, but at the time I got a call from Paul, whom I barely knew.

"I hear you're talking about me behind my back," he said, just short of a snarl. "Don't try to deny it, Alicia told me."

"Well, Alicia does love her drama," I replied. "But there's nothing I said to her that I wouldn't say directly to you, given that you acted irresponsibly with another close friend of mine."

"That's none of your business."

"Listen, Alicia loves to create scenes like this. But I'm not sorry for trying to warn her about somebody with whom she's getting involved, if another friend, whom she also knows, has had a bad experience."

"I've always tried to reach out to you, to be your friend, but apparently you have a hard time having male friends," Paul said, clearly trying to get a rise out of me.

"Listen, Paul. We really don't know each other. I have plenty of male friends, but you are not one of them. I'm sorry if I hurt you in any way, but perhaps you should be more responsible in your dealings with people, and we wouldn't be having this conversation."

With that, I hung up. A couple weeks later, Alicia ended her association with Paul. Today Alicia and I are still friends. But every time I see Paul, I feel the need to apologize. While, strictly speaking, I wasn't engaging in frivolous gossip, I can't say my motives were completely pure. What I was saying about Paul (obviously not his real name) was true. He later became the one yoga teacher with a circulating e-mail list among women asking if they had been groped by him. But while I was concerned about Alicia, I wasn't exactly rooting for her success with Paul, either.

The point is that I had spoken about Paul and now I had to live with the results of that every time I ran into him. Finally, four years later, when I saw him I took the opportunity to formally apologize.

"Listen, Paul," I said. "I just want to say that things got a bit funky between us a couple years ago. Essentially, Alicia started seeing both of us at the same time. You had had your experience with Suzanne, which she was pretty broken up about. It was pretty confusing. I just want to apologize for my half of it."

"No problem," he said tersely. He looked at me with barely disguised distaste. He didn't apologize.

But it didn't matter. I had finally owned my half of the drama. I had apologized and was free of the connection. When you apologize for wrongdoing, you become liberated from the negative charge. Whether or not that person accepts your apology, if it is sincere, you are released from the negative connection. You become free.

There is an old story about a student who went to a sage and asked him to talk to him about gossip, with which he struggled within himself. How could he prevent himself from speaking about people behind their backs? The sage told the man to take a feather pillow out into the town square and to rip it open, spreading the feathers to the wind. Then he should come back to him when he was finished.

The student went out to the square and tore open the pillow. The wind picked up the feathers, scattering them throughout the town and beyond.

"Okay, I have done what you have asked. But I don't see how that is going to help me," the student said to his teacher.

"Now then," said the teacher, "go and collect all the feathers."

The student looked at his teacher and immediately understood. It was impossible to undo what had been done. To collect all the words he had spoken was impossible. They were dust in the wind.

"It is much easier to hurt a person by speaking than by not speaking," said the sage.

This gave the student a moment to pause before speaking. It always gives me pause whenever I am tempted to hold forth with an opinion, which can slide into a judgment.

Think about it terms of connectivity. Your word is a physical entity and has a physical effect. It is made up of waves that enter into somebody else's ear, vibrates their tympanum, and physically *changes them*. It is energy, pure and simple. It is an element of consciousness, and like all things, it is connected to the whole. It is an extension and an emissary of yourself.

Send it forth into the world with integrity and love.

# ADVICE

## Give and Receive with Caution

The function of a liberated man isn't to scold or to
harangue; it's to delight them back to their senses. . . .
Their Eros, connected to body and self.

ALAN WATTS

One of the more difficult aspects of relationship is watching people you love suffer in a bad one. How many times
have we watched a good friend stay in an unhappy relationship, only to leave it and end up in another? How many
times has that person been ourselves? And isn't it so much
easier to see it in other people than in ourselves?

So what do you do if you see your loved ones in the
throes of agony, in a bitter relationship that doesn't bring
out the best in either of them? What do you do when they
complain and complain, over and over, about their partner?

Do you give them advice?

I have a rule that I try to adhere to, with mixed results:

I don't give advice to friends anymore. This hasn't always been the case. When I was young, as a congenital know-it-all, I was always giving advice. Later, as I matured and developed a fair amount of discernment, it got even worse. I could "see" what was going on with other people and I wouldn't hesitate to hold forth with my wisdom.

But even when I was right, I was wrong. Most times my friends just needed to talk things out with a sympathetic ear. I remember one case where my friend George was having a really hard time with his girlfriend. He had asked for a trial separation, and they weren't seeing each other.

"This girl doesn't know how to have any fun. I mean, it's all about talking about the relationship . . . what are we doing . . . where are we going? Blah, blah, blah . . ."

"That sounds hard," I said cautiously. A mere month ago, he'd been raving about how great she was.

"She just can't be present, you know? Her mind is going all the time. She's super-critical and judgmental. She's also so insecure that she's insanely jealous. I'm just not having a good time here." George sighed. "She's not who I thought she was. I'm thinking of ending it for good."

"It doesn't sound like much fun."

George nodded. "I'm just done with this bullshit. I'm going to end it."

"Maybe you should," I said.

A week later George had reunited with his girlfriend and he called me up because he said he wanted to get something off his chest.

"You know, Arthur, I've got a real bone to pick with you."

"Really? What?"

"You didn't support me in my relationship."

"I didn't?"

"No. You didn't. You've been negative about it all along."

"I have?"

"Yes. And I really want to make this work. I really do. She's a special person. Going through a hard time right now, but she's worth it."

"I just want you to be happy and I support you completely," I said.

We talked about it some more, and I didn't try to argue with him. It was just a good example of what can happen when you give advice to somebody in the throes of a difficult relationship.

Six months later they broke up for good.

So, what are you supposed to do when you see somebody else's issues clearly? What are you supposed to do with all that discernment you've developed over the years?

Sometimes the height of wisdom is to keep quiet. Discerning an incompatibility or seeing through a manipulation is a great ability; it takes knowledge of human nature and behavior. But not pointing it out to a friend who is suffering takes true wisdom.

Telling the truth to somebody who's not ready to hear it can be unloving.

In our society we are taught that "tough love" is sometimes the way to go. But is it really effective? Or is the longer, slower process of listening and helping to guide a person to their own conclusions more effective than simply holding forth with your opinion?

Believe me, I am as opinionated as they come. But I have

found that no matter how much I've been articulate and clear in my opinion, especially when it regards other people's relationships, they rarely have moved an inch in any direction before they were emotionally good and ready. And the problem with giving an opinion is that it's impossible not to be invested in it. It's human nature to want to be right. And as soon as you are invested in being right, you have tossed all your freedom out the window.

If someone actually *asks* you for your opinion, it's a different story. But even then, proceed with caution. It is not easy to tell difficult truths to people in a way that ensures they will be heard.

In a realization of the dharma, you accept all things as they are. This means letting go of control, even letting go of the desire to try to alleviate somebody else's suffering, the cause of which may even be obvious to you. The level to which you try to control somebody is directly commensurate to the amount of freedom you have. More control equals less freedom for you.

Simply listening with a sympathetic ear is the most powerfully healing thing you can do. And it inserts no ego, creates no investment in the outcome, and does no harm.

# PARTNERING
# WITH ALL

## The Beloved Loving Itself

*Look at you, you madman,*
*Screaming you are thirsty*
*And are dying in a desert*
*When all around you there is nothing but water!*

KABIR

What is the difference between romantic love, which is the love between two people, and divine love, the love between different aspects of consciousness?

With romantic love, you are focusing all your attention on one other person. They are special, therefore you love them—you reserve your love for them. The rest of the people in the world are not special and not deserving of this special kind of love. And how can you possibly love people you don't know in the same way that you love your family or your lover or your spouse?

With divine love, you are not simply partnering with one person, you are partnering with all of creation. Through losing identification with your small self, the "I" completely disappears. You, as a manifestation of consciousness, are "seeing God with God's eyes." There is no *you* to love, and there is no *object* to be loved. There is just consciousness (God, Atman, Brahman, or whatever culturally comfortable term we have for expressing all that is) endlessly loving itself.

This can start on an interpersonal level between two lovers; stare into the eyes of your beloved and you can get your first taste of nonduality. There is no me. There is no you. There is just a sense of *being,* which manifests itself as peacefulness and love.

In fact, what many people mistake for desire or lust or love or connectedness is actually a moment of pure forgetting in which the small self completely disappears, providing, for an immaculate instant, a sense of profound connection and freedom in which love, the true nature of things, is revealed. Instead of keeping your eye on your partner and on what he or she is doing or not doing, you keep your eye on love itself.

You can take it a step further. Your lover is not just an external manifestation of you, reflecting you, but in the deepest spiritual sense, that person *is* you. If everything we see, feel, and hear is one blast of consciousness, how is your partner, as a manifestation of this consciousness, separate from you? Like Jung's collective unconscious or a dream in which we are playing all the roles, our partners are doing that in our waking life—one mind loving itself.

It's all simply consciousness having a conversation with itself, whether it is in the form of you and your lover locked in the heat of passion, or of trees blowing in a breeze.

Look deeply at your partner and see yourself.

Change your perspective and become free of self entirely.

When we are free of identification with the small self, when we don't draw our identity from who we think we are, then the mind, the finite entity creating apparent separation from the larger Self, God, or Consciousness, loses its grip. In this way, all fear and separation is released and a sense of merging occurs.

There's nothing to be afraid of, because *we are not separate from anything.* We are different, but not separate.

This connectedness and the added connectedness of sex is what the spiritual teacher Osho calls a *vertical* experience. A vertical experience is one in which horizontal time disappears. During the absolute NOW of laughter, orgasm, meditation, or even a good sneeze, there is no future and no past. This experience is not limited; it is available all the time. A lover is unnecessary to our experiencing this taste of oneness, this love, the same way a partner is unnecessary for dancing. You can dance alone, with the entire world as your partner. Everything you rest your gaze upon becomes an opportunity to express love.

To quote Kahlil Gibran, when you look at everything as the beloved, you become the lover and the loved, the gaze and the object being gazed upon. This is ultimately what we are searching for, what we get a taste of when we meet that special person who releases those strong feelings in us. But we don't need them, we already have access to this infinite love, as close as our own breath. We only have to realize it.

Even when the conditioning is intense, even when you have identified it and know it inside and out, even when you have chosen the exact person with whom to play it out, know there is no such thing as "looking for love in all the wrong places." It's all God.

This is divine love.

What is discovered in this awareness is the difference between romantic love and divine love, which has a lot to do with the difference between being alone and loneliness. Loneliness is the absence of somebody, a negative state. Aloneness can include the full and vibrant presence of oneself. In loneliness we are *seeking love;* in aloneness we are simply *expressing love.* In divine love we are already full and have no expectations of others to fulfill us.

And in divine love, you are an irreplaceable manifestation of consciousness, *you can never be alone.* You are merged with all. Feel that and never be lonely.

So, are we supposed to give up on romantic love, with all its beautiful tastes of freedom and madness? No, it is just another phenomenon and one of the portals, but not the only portal, into divine love. It is a beautiful phenomenon, but it is not necessary to our experience of true freedom, happiness, and love.

And it can be a form of bondage, just like any other attachment.

Romantic love, with all its attendant highs and lows, is the burning ground. But even within its flames can be the realization that you are both the fire and the object being burned.

All is fine.

# PART TWO

# Right Before

## First Approaches into Your Orbit

# WHERE'S YOUR PARTNER?

## Meet Them Anywhere, Anytime

We do not see things as they are.
We see them as we are.

THE TALMUD

Sometimes it can seem like you will never find the love of your dreams.

So let go of the dream.

You may be chasing your conditioned idea of what your partner should look like, what they do for a living, and what kind of body they have. He should be tall and muscular. She should be thin and cosmopolitan. You tell yourself you're going to hold out for the right person, damn it!

So how do you find this person?

Aside from the ideas we have discussed about expanding our ability to love by becoming more *loving* and thus attracting a loving mirror, is there anything else we can do to move things along?

The answer is everything and nothing.

If you are not looking for something outside of yourself to make you happy, if you have moved beyond the fairytale conditioning of being rescued from your life, if you are truly open to a relationship, then the possibilities are endless. The person with whom you could be happy might be standing right in front of you in line at the grocery counter or putting their mat down next to you in a yoga class.

So how do you meet somebody without being in constant "cruise" mode?

By being awake and meeting each person fully in the moment.

By meeting the entire world as that special somebody.

Eventually the world will begin to take notice.

It's as simple as that.

# FIRST MEETING

## Just Breathe

The mind, the Buddha, living creatures—
these are not three different things.

*AVATAMASAKA SUTRA*

You're taking Fido out to the dog park one day and a beautiful woman arrives with her pooch. You're smitten beyond anything you've experienced before, and when she smiles at you, you're thrown into a state of paralysis.

Or you're browsing in a bookstore and the good-looking man across the way is looking at you, trying to catch your eye. You're attracted and you suddenly feel nervous. He's walking toward you as all the words fall out of your head and you can't even remember your own name.

How do you deal with the nervousness that can arise when you're truly attracted to somebody and you want to make a connection, but have no idea how? And beyond that, your tongue seems to have swollen to the size of your liver?

This response is common. It is equal parts biological and social conditioning, with a good dose of your personal "story" thrown in for good measure.

But let's break it down a bit. What is really happening when you see somebody who takes your breath away and makes your knees week? Has anything changed in that moment? Aren't you still in the bookstore, holding your book? Aren't you still walking your dog? Nothing has actually changed except that you've been triggered. But that's like saying nothing's changed except for that arrow shot through your chest. It's not particularly helpful.

Still, you don't have to *do* anything as nervousness and desire arise and momentarily engulf your worldview. Remember, nothing is happening except what is happening in your mind. Thoughts arise like *She's beautiful. He's checking me out!* And can quickly become *She's too good-looking for me.* Or *I'm not pretty enough for him.* Or *He looks like a player.* Or *She's just one of those women who needs attention all the time. I'm not going to put myself in a place to be rejected!*

All this can be happening in a split second. Before you know it, you're walking up to the person and saying, "Who the hell do you think you are?"

This is an exaggeration, but not by much.

The mind can get into a whirlwind. It can go to past experiences and say this is what's going to happen now. It can travel to the future and play out all sorts of scenarios. The mind will do anything except be with the reality of *what is,* which is simply the arising of attraction.

Still, when the butterflies are doing loop-the-loops in your stomach and you've suddenly lost the ability to speak, what can you do? The first thing to do is take a deep breath. Slowly let it out. Then take another one. Slowly let that one out. Let yourself get grounded in the moment.

Then come into a witnessing position with the thoughts that are arising. Watch them. Breathe and witness. Witness and breathe.

What is actually at stake here? You were fine before the sighting of the person who triggered the feelings, and you will be fine afterwards. View the desire that is arising as a beautiful thing—you are alive! But don't let it completely swamp your screen of awareness. Keep some perspective; you will live either way. The only thing that has happened is that desire has arisen and give birth to a series of thoughts in your mind. Otherwise, things are exactly the same, *because nothing has actually happened outside of your own perceptions.*

On a deeper level, you are meeting another manifestation of creation, another chip of consciousness. They have all the hopes, dreams, and fears   perhaps about different things—that you have, because they too are human. Keep a "same-same" awareness. They are probably not judging you because they are too busy hoping that you're not judging them.

So there is nothing to prove here. The attraction, on your part, is already there. Did the other person have to do anything to initiate it? No. They just were *being.* The same is true for you. There is nothing you need to do to engender attraction. Don't try. Just be. Because there is nothing you need to prove, you can take the pressure off yourself.

What if you don't consider yourself an attractive person? Don't you need to try harder? Of course, while personality and intelligence come into play and make somebody more or less attractive, isn't chemistry independent of looks? How many times have you met a beautiful person and not felt chemistry? And how many times have you felt chemistry for the quirky, offbeat, and not traditionally beautiful person?

For every person there is somebody in the world who will find them attractive. There is somebody for everybody. So stop trying so hard.

Once, after a play, I met a woman I was attracted to. It was a bit of a setup because a mutual friend had said she thought we would get along and that she wanted to introduce us. She didn't tell the woman, who was acting in the play, because she didn't want to make it seem too obvious. The play was a comedy about religious belief, and she was terrific in it. I was struck by her classic beauty. When she came out afterward, we were introduced as part of a group, and I immediately began talking about the play, the playwright, spirituality, belief, the book I was writing, blah, blah, blah . . .

Instead of trusting the moment, I felt that I had something to prove. It turns out she had started seeing somebody and wasn't available anyway, so all my machinations to show how clever I was proved to be irrelevant. We all do this at some point, painting a picture that says *I'm valuable.* See how smart I am? Or how much money I make? Or . . . Fill in the blank.

But what is the concept of *value* in a human being? Are you not valuable simply because you *exist?* And at a deeper level, in spite of what society would have us believe, aren't all people *equally valuable?* It's funny to talk about this principle in relation to meeting a potential date, but it applies. Our society, with its obsession with external power and celebrity, tells us that some people are more valuable than others. Some people are "stars" and others aren't. And if you're not a star, then you don't rate. This idea is absolutely false and ego-based.

This outlook is what causes the anxiety in the moment: the concept or idea or conditioning that we somehow may not measure up in the eyes of the other. That some people are more valuable than others is something that is drummed into us in our competitive society. But this comparison and judgment and competition create a separation from our fellow human beings that is the source of much suffering.

Everybody is equally valuable simply because they exist. When you strip away all the conditioning, education, money, and so on, what is left? The same humanity and spark that is in everybody—none is more valuable than another.

The beauty and wonder of human existence is that no matter where we are born, or into what culture, all of us have similar aspirations toward love, family, and spirituality. They may seem very different from one another, but all possess innate *humanness*. When you see how we are all the same instead of how we are different, you realize there is nothing you need to do to make yourself lovable.

You already are.

# FIRST DATE

## No Expectations

I never expect anything from anyone,
and therefore I am never disappointed.

PARAMAHANSA YOGANANDA

A close friend of mine named Leslie, who's thirty-three, flew to New York City recently. While standing outside the JFK terminal, she wondered out loud how long the line for a taxi was going to take. A man about fifteen years older than she offered her a ride in the limo he was taking into the city, courtesy of his publisher. Leslie, tall, blond, and beautiful, was always getting these kinds of offers. After checking him out and looking at the limo, she said, "Sure, why not."

It turns out that Jim was in New York from Los Angeles to pitch an idea for his second book to his editor. Leslie was there visiting friends. They hit it off in the limo, talking about everything and nothing. Leslie thought that he was a nice guy who seemed humble in spite of having published a moderately successful book. Once in the city, they swapped cell-phone numbers and went their separate ways. Leslie said he should call her and tell her how his meeting went.

The next day Jim called and said his meeting went well, and asked Leslie if she wanted to get together to celebrate. They agreed to meet in the lobby of the hotel where Jim was staying. When he got there, he was in a business suit and wanted to change, and invited Leslie up to the suite. She felt comfortable enough with him to go, talking to him through the door separating the bedroom from the sitting room, as he told her to call the concierge and set up a dinner reservation. When he came out, freshly changed, they talked some more and he joked about feeling like they'd known each other forever.

Then he tried to kiss her.

Because Leslie was in no way ready to be kissed, she pushed him away with a joke.

"Dive right in, why don't you!" she said dryly.

"I'm sorry," Jim said. "But you're just so irresistible."

"I'm afraid you're going to have to resist."

Luckily for her, he was a gentleman and they went out to dinner. They had a good time, drank a lot of wine, and ended up at a bar around the corner from the apartment where Leslie was staying.

"Thank you for a wonderful evening," she said.

"Don't you want to come back to the hotel and have a nightcap?"

"I'm staying two blocks from here. I think I'll just walk home."

Jim gave it the old college try, but Leslie was firm. He walked her to her door and they said good night.

The next day Jim called wanting to see Leslie again that evening. By now the friends whom Leslie was meeting were in town. They were the reason she had traveled to New York. When she suggested that they talk back in Los Angeles, Jim got irritated and slightly pushy.

By this time Leslie was getting turned off. When she got back to Los Angeles, she never returned Jim's calls.

Jim made the common mistake of having expectations. He expected, because Leslie was fun and easygoing, that she was going to sleep with him on the first date. But Leslie isn't the airhead Jim might have assumed she was. I've known her a long time, and she is bubbly and effervescent and can be skittish on a bad day, but all the time she's watching very carefully what is going on and how people are reacting to her. Many a time Leslie has come up with astute observations of the people around her.

Leslie felt that Jim really liked her, but over the course of their first date, she saw signs of his ego rearing its head. And during the date he had major expectations. Here was this friendly, beautiful, sexy woman who had accompanied him to his hotel room. Obviously she wanted to have sex with him right away. Whatever mistakes Leslie made here (and I think she made several obvious ones regarding her safety with a stranger), Jim was not reading her correctly at all.

On a first date there are going to be all sorts of expectations, hopes, and fears. Will she like me? Will he think I'm pretty? Will there be any chemistry at all? All of those questions prevent you from just relaxing into the moment with what is happening. Leslie said she gave no indication at all to Jim that she wanted to kiss him in the hotel room. She was bundled up in jeans and a sweater, showing no flesh.

Jim was perhaps taking the situation—strange woman in his hotel room—and extrapolating from there, drawing the wrong conclusion. At the end of the night he didn't stop, either. He tried to get her back to the hotel.

Leslie, who'd been in a long-term relationship and wasn't current on the rules of dating, sincerely asked me if people were sleeping together on the first date these days, or if she was shutting him down too quickly when he kept calling her during her entire stay in New York. I said no, he wasn't hearing her clearly or respecting what she wanted. Instead of making a connection with a woman he liked, he ended up by alienating her completely.

On a first date, be as you are in any situation, treating every moment as if it were blooming fresh. As soon as you are in the land of expectation, you are not present in the moment with what is. Rather, you are seeing only what you want to see.

Try instead to approach a first date (and life in general) with a sense of play, for in meeting the world with a sense of play, you are present with what is, whether it is suffering or joy. You have no agenda, you are innocent. I would say that, more than anything else, spirituality embodies a fluid sense of play, because play can only happen in the moment, as can authentic emotion. I am speaking about play from its most ordinary form to its most exalted. One of the reasons we are attracted to professional athletes, musicians, and actors is that they are completely absorbed, playing in the moment. They are accessing their joy—passionate, intense, and emotional, letting the full range of experience be felt right now.

But play can be experienced in more-ordinary exchanges, whether in buying groceries, ordering from a waiter, or paying for a cab. In fact, every exchange with another human being is an opportunity to play and to connect with some-body in the moment, whether through a smile, a gesture, or a word. But this can only be done when we are not ob-sessing about the past or having an agenda about the future. Because the truth is we don't have any idea about what the future brings. None.

Right now, as I write this, I am preparing to meet a woman with whom I've been corresponding with by e-mail for six months. We met online and she lives in Los Angeles, but is staying in Texas while she tries to finish a novel and work things out with an on-again-off-again relationship (we met online during one of the "off" cycles). We decided to be friends. We both enjoy our e-mail interaction, as we are both writers and take pains to amuse each other. We've never met, and have only spoken on the phone to make the dinner plans we have for tonight. I had chosen a casual but nice Italian restaurant. Annie just called and wanted to upgrade to the outdoor garden at Chateau Marmont, a hip, overpriced hotel, so she could have a cigarette after her meal. She said it was a little more expensive but she wouldn't eat much, implying that I was going to pay.

Hmmmm . . . are we on a date all of a sudden? We hadn't spoken about the status of her relationship for months, keeping our conversations to our mutual interests of books, movies, and the state of the world.

Regarding dinner, I said I didn't really care, but if we were going to spend that kind of money, why not go to Orso, which had better food?

I left it in her hands to find a place she wanted to go.

I have no idea what is going to happen. I have no idea what the situation is with her relationship. Our correspondence has been platonic the entire time, and I have had no agenda to turn it into something else.

But what is going on? What is going to happen tonight?

This is a situation in which there is absolutely no choice but to have no expectations. When you don't know the terrain you are entering, which is the case with most first dates, then it is best to bring your awareness into the present moment, where you can be most awake.

So now I step into the unknown, where it is imperative to have no expectations in order to see reality clearly.

THE STRANGENESS of meeting somebody with whom you've exchanged countless e-mails but have never met can't be underestimated. Getting to know somebody on the purest level of mind, without the distorting aspects of the physical, is an interesting process. It almost takes us back to another era when people corresponded via letter over great distance and periods of time.

When I knock on the door of the friend's house where Annie is staying, I have no idea what to expect. I've only seen one picture, which was a black-and-white headshot in which she looked ravishing. When the door opened, the first thing I noticed was her coat, which was sleeveless and very furry. Annie was pretty in an all-American way, and looked nothing like her picture. We smiled at each other.

"How weird is this?" I said, laughing.

"Totally," she replied. Her voice was a nasal twang.

I was relieved that I was attracted to Annie, but not overwhelmed with desire. That always makes it easier. As we drove to the restaurant, we chatted about various topics and kept glancing at each other and smiling. During dinner we kept up the banter until I asked her why she was in Los

Angeles, making a sudden trip from Texas. Wasn't she supposed to be finishing her novel and wasn't she involved with a script that her boyfriend was going to direct?

"That's a whole other story," Annie sighed. She proceeded to tell me about her relationship with her boyfriend, who is actively addicted to alcohol and drugs. "He's great seventy percent of the time, but the other thirty percent is a nightmare . . . the two-day benders, the meanness, the lies . . . waking up to an empty bed. I'm too old for this."

We spent most of the dinner talking about how she was going to deal with this man she loved who was a raging alcoholic, but who didn't feel that he had any problem at all. I listened sympathetically, offering advice from my own experience with active addicts, outlining the whole dynamic of codependence and referring her to Al-Anon programs so she could start to figure out her part in it.

Annie nodded and said she didn't know what to do. She didn't want to talk about it with her family and friends, all of whom loved her boyfriend. She started to cry and then looked me in the eye, thanking me for being there for the last seven months, writing and offering her advice and listening to her.

"It's pathetic, I know," she said, wiping away a tear. "But you were the only person I felt I could talk to. The only person who I felt didn't judge me, a total stranger. It was such a ray of light at times when it got very gloomy. Thank you."

This was an unexpected turn for our first dinner. She had mentioned she was having trouble with her boyfriend, but not for quite a while. I was expecting more good-natured bantering along the lines of our e-mails, but this was what was up.

"I've got to leave, but I'm not sure I can. It might take a while."

"Yes, you might have to do some more research, right?"

Annie looked at me and laughed. I told her about the time I was with a friend whose father had died of alcoholism. We were passing a drunk clutching a bottle of cheap whiskey in his hand while begging for money, slurring his words.

"Yup, just doing some more research here. Yup, booze really can be bad for you," my friend said in reference to the drunken man on the street.

Andrea laughed ruefully. The check came and I grabbed it. She didn't protest. Two weeks later she was back in Texas, trying again with her boyfriend. A week after that, she packed up and moved out.

You never really know what is going on with another person whom you have just met. Many times it's impossible even to know what's happening with people you have known for years. So, on a first date, anything can happen.

It might be a date, it might be a casual dinner to get to know somebody because the word "date" is too scary for some people, and it might be the first meal you have with your future spouse. But you never know what is going to happen because you don't know who the other person is and what you might mean to them. After straightening out the fact that we were going to be friends, I thought Annie and I were casual and fun pen pals; it turns out that my correspondence with her was much more meaningful than that.

It turned out that our "date," which I thought was going to be fun and platonic, a continuation of our acerbic e-mails, or perhaps *maybe* romantic, was meant to be much more heartfelt and healing.

There is nothing to do when meeting somebody for the

first time but *meet them,* in the moment, without expectation of what should be.

It is only in *accepting,* rather than *expecting,* that you can actually find out what the relationship is supposed to be, whether it is that of acquaintance, friend, or the love of your life.

# NONATTACHMENT

## Love Can Only Happen Right Now

You must live in the present,
launch yourself on every wave,
find your eternity in
each moment.

HENRY DAVID THOREAU

One of my closest friends is a former girlfriend named Amber. An ex-model, she is still a jet-setter who seems to have a knack for finding herself in the exact right place at the right time, going from one fabulous trip to another incredible adventure. Her love life is strewn with dead bodies, and she herself has suffered in several incredibly dysfunctional relationships. She is currently in a long and brutal on-again-off-again relationship with Ted, a penniless alcoholic, to whom she is sexually addicted. Ted is very obsessive and jealous, often flying into uncontrollable rages, but stopping short of physical violence.

Recently, when Amber was in Paris with friends, taking a break from Ted, she ran into Ossam, a friend of a friend. He is a very wealthy Turkish man whose family is in charge of supplying electricity to much of the Middle East. But Ossam's real passion is sailboats. Amber had only met Ossam once before, when they had a fling in Italy; they didn't stay in touch. But here they were, now both in Paris. Ossam invited Amber back to Turkey to sail with him on his new boat after he finished up some business in London. Amber agreed.

Four days later, Amber set off from Paris to Istanbul. She ran into trouble with her visa, but was helped by a kind Turkish man who negotiated it for her. She was then met by Ossam's driver, who took her to another terminal, where she flew on to a port town on the Aegean Sea. She was met by a young man who crewed on the boat, and they took a one-hour cab ride to another town.

"That is your boat," the young man said, pointing to a beautiful 120-foot sailing yacht moored in the harbor. Amber was tired from traveling ten hours, but the sun was setting and the yachts bobbing in the harbor were enchanting. She was excited, but also a bit nervous to be so far from home with somebody who was essentially a complete stranger.

"I will have to say good-bye to you now, because once we are on the boat, I will not be able to talk to you as we have been talking," the young man said, as they walked to the wharf. He shook her hand formally. "It was very nice to meet you, and I very much enjoyed our conversation."

With that, they got on the boat that ferried them toward the fabulous yacht. When they boarded, the vessel seemed to be empty and dark. The young man, carrying Amber's bag, motioned her to follow him. With some apprehension, she did, entering the main salon.

It was filled with dozens of candles, which burnished the teak and brass fittings.

"Hello, Amber," a voice said. The room was filled with roses, and the man was obscured in shadow, so she didn't see him right away. He stood up; it was Ossam, dressed in white linen. "Welcome, my dear."

"Oh my God." Amber was struck speechless by it all, by the romance and beauty of the yacht, the candles, the harbor, Ossam—everything.

"Champagne?" Ossam asked. And then they both started laughing at the sheer perfection of it all, like something out of a movie. It broke the tension. Ossam opened the champagne and they started talking and never stopped. The chef appeared and took their order for a five-course meal. They talked and laughed until three in the morning, at which point Ossam carried Amber into the master cabin, where they made love.

Ossam had made tentative plans for other friends to join them on the five-day cruise around the Mediterranean, but he never called them. It was just Ossam and Amber and a five-person crew to cater to their every need. They ate and swam and talked and made love. They sailed all night under a full moon. On the third day, Ossam, who loved to fish, put out five lines over the stern of the boat.

"You maybe catch one fish a month here," he said. "There are no more fish in this part of the sea."

An hour later the crew started yelling. Four of the five lines had tuna on them; it was like a miracle from the gods! They ate tuna for the rest of the trip. In harmony with each other and with the sea, they created heaven with each other.

They poured each other's hearts out to each other, but they never spoke of a future together. They were in the NOW, which was providing them with a peak experience.

When it came time for Amber to leave, she held it together until she got to the airport, where she broke down sobbing. What was happening between them? Could they ever be together? Would she ever see him again? She told me she would move to Turkey to be with Ossam, but they hadn't spoken about it. After she cried, she just decided that the only way to deal with it was to let it go.

"I am the type of person where you will be going about your day in Los Angeles and turn around and I will be there," Ossam wrote to her after she left.

No promises were made. But how was Amber supposed to deal with this situation? After such an incredible experience, how do you let it go?

This is where the principle of nonattachment comes in. An experience isn't a prison, nor is it a contract. So have the experiences that you have in the world without expecting them to last forever. Sometimes they might lead to a lasting relationship, sometimes they won't. But in order to enjoy them at all, it is important to simply experience them in the moment. Amber has a memory that will last a lifetime, but she could easily ruin subsequent moments by dreaming her life away about that brief idyll. Looking to experience it again or to re-create it, she could lose out on the present moment, which is *the only livable moment*. The NOW is the only moment in which life is created. The rest is memory or futurizing.

The same is true for negative experiences, which Amber had on her arrival back in Los Angeles. Although she had broken up with Ted, she had let him stay in her apartment during the month she was gone, during which time he had read all of her journals. When she got back, he was in a rage about perceived affairs she had had while they were together.

The second night Amber was home, Ted got so drunk that he decided he was going to kill himself. He got in his car and drove to her house, intending to crash on the way. When he didn't, he let himself into her apartment. Amber woke up to find him standing above her in a glowering rage.

"You fucking bitch," he slurred. "I'm going to kill you. Tonight is the night you die."

He attacked Amber, holding her down. He put his hands around her neck and began choking her. She pleaded for her life and cried. He held her hostage, alternately choking her and berating her for two long hours. Amber tried to stay calm and talk Ted down, to no avail. She didn't think she would survive it, until he finally passed out.

Within the space of two days, Amber had a peak experience and a horrible experience, both around the polarities of love. We had a long conversation and I encouraged her to call a battered-women's shelter and get some advice and support.

"You know, if you look at this as a metaphor for the kind of relationship you want, you have a choice," I said. "You can choose the version of love and romance you experienced in Turkey, or you can choose to re-create the drama and violence of your childhood. The two are clearly outlined for you."

As the song goes, it's a bitter line between love and hate. The first suspect in most murders is immediately the spouse;

strong emotions can flip and descend into violence. Amber's father was an alcoholic who flew into drunken rages, forcing her mother to take Amber out in the middle of the night, where they would drive around until dawn and her father had passed out. The choices presented to Amber now, whether she was going to repeat this childhood experience in her life or move on to a different definition of love, couldn't have been more clearly demonstrated.

Both of these experiences have pointed up useful ways to practice nonattachment, either to a beautiful experience or to a horrific one.

Everything in life is fleeting, and nothing lasts forever—neither the sublime nor the horrible. So don't trade your happiness for either one.

# SEDUCTION

## Flirting versus Manipulation

*I wouldn't coax the plant if I were you.*
*Such watchful nurturing may do it harm.*
*Let the soil rest from so much digging*
*And wait until it's dry before you water it.*
*The leaf's inclined to find its own direction;*
*Give it a chance to seek the sunlight for itself.*

*Much growth is stunted by too-careful prodding*
*Too-eager tenderness.*
*The things we love we have to learn to leave alone.*

NAOMI LONG MADGETT

We grow up with a lot of mythology around the idea of romantic love, starting with the rich and handsome prince who's going to rescue the beautiful maiden. The Cinderella story is so ingrained in our psyche that men and women often act out this role without intending to, as Amber's experience with Ossam demonstrated. As we meet each other in the romantic marketplace, we all can resort to culturally prescribed roles in order to make ourselves more attractive. In women it can manifest as hyper-femininity, exaggerating the false ideals of passivity, sexual seductiveness, or helplessness. For men the roles show up as displays of money or power. Both roles are not taking into account the actual person standing in front of them. Nor are they taking into account their own deeper needs.

A close friend of mine, Ashley, who has long, strawberry blond hair and an equally long history of breaking men's hearts, was standing in line at the bank one day, the picture of slender California beauty. Divorced, she hadn't ever really supported herself. She lives in a condo that her mother owns, and she pays nominal rent. She works part-time and is in the process of trying to find herself and her path. None of this, of course, stops men from throwing themselves at her.

"Excuse me." A tall, well-dressed man was approaching her, holding a check in his hand. "I just didn't know who else to share this with. Can I show you something?"

Ashley looked around. She was in the middle of a Malibu bank in broad daylight, so she was hoping she wasn't going to be flashed, as she had been two weeks before on the street.

"Um . . . okay."

"Look at this," the man said. "I just don't have anybody else to share this with. I'm a lawyer and I just won a big case."

With that, he showed Ashley, a complete stranger, a check for $250,000. For a divorced woman who traditionally dated older, wealthier men, this was like showing red meat to a lioness. Plus he was attractive and fun. They started talking while they waited in line, and the man, Frank, invited Ashley to lunch, where he ordered oysters and an expensive bottle of champagne. They got tipsy and shared a lot of laughs on a Friday afternoon in Malibu.

Ashley is thirty-three and divorced. Frank is forty-eight, never married, with no children. Neither of these facts slowed either of them down. After they finished lunch, fueled on champagne and money, they wandered around some boutiques and Frank bought Ashley a scarf, a pair of boots, and lots of beauty supplies. When they got back to the car, Frank and Ashley kissed like teenagers for fifteen minutes. They made plans to see each other for dinner the following night.

The next night, Ashley and Frank went to Geoffrey's, a famously romantic restaurant overlooking the ocean in Malibu. Under a full moon glistening over the water, they had a great time and ended up spending the night together. So far, aside from moving quickly into a physical relationship, there was nothing out of the ordinary. Then, after they'd had sex, Frank wanted to know how many orgasms she'd had.

"I don't know . . . I mean, it was good."

"Good? Just good?" Frank insisted on more information. "But how many orgasms did you have?"

Ashley laughed it off and said enough. But Frank was obsessive. He wanted to know, and persisted until she told him. Two.

"We're going to have to work on that, get that number up there."

"Fine with me," Ashley said, feeling a bit weird.

The next night they went out again, to another fabulous

restaurant in Malibu. Frank gave her the latest Motorola cell phone because Ashley had mentioned she was looking for one.

"You know, you don't have to buy me so much stuff," Ashley said, thoroughly enjoying all the stuff he bought her.

"I'm in love with you." Frank said with no preamble, in the middle of dinner.

"Right," Ashley said, not certain how to take it.

"Do you want me to call my mother right now?" Frank said. "I will. You can talk to her. Tell her I've met the woman of my dreams."

"That won't be necessary . . . I . . . Look, there's something I need to tell you." Ashley paused. "I'm still getting out of a relationship. It's over, but we made plans to go to Europe for the holidays, and I'm leaving next week for two weeks."

"What? But . . ." Frank was stunned. "You're going to Europe with him? Why?"

"It's just . . . I can't cancel, I can't do it to him. We made these plans and he's bought the tickets."

"But you're my girlfriend." Frank began laughing at the statement, and then suddenly there were tears in his eyes. He began to laugh and cry at the same time, putting on quite a display.

"I'm not your girlfriend," she said, looking around the restaurant, concerned and not a little embarrassed.

"This is not the story I'm going to tell our children about the way we met—that their mother ran off to Europe with another man!" Frank's voice was rising. "I want to take you to Aspen for the holidays."

"I'm sorry. I—"

"Give me this man's number, I'll call him and pay him back for the ticket to Europe."

"That's really not the point."

"Are you using me to make this other man jealous? Or . . . or using him to make me jealous?"

"No! I'm just . . . just . . . confused," Ashley stuttered.

It went on like that for the entire dinner, Frank using every trick he could think of in order to get what he thought he wanted. Over the next few days he called Ashley obsessively. And when she went to Europe he was bitterly disappointed.

This is an extreme example of manipulation on both sides, but particularly with Frank. Now Ashley has her behavior to look at as well, something that she started to do after the whole debacle. She is the ultimate escape artist, always promising men the moon as long as no emotions are involved, then disappearing when men have any expectations that she will follow up on the promises her behavior implies. It is a way in which she punishes the men who are attracted to her beauty—a long history of seduction and abandonment. As long as things are kept casual in the seductive part of the courtship, then she will show up and be available. As soon as the man gives up part of his heart, it's time to bring on the punishment, usually by withdrawing. In this way she is a bit addicted to the infatuation stage of relationship—addicted to the high.

Still, it's easy to see that Frank is completely unbalanced. From the beginning, he was using money in an obvious way to attract Ashley's attention; the subtext had become easy-to-read text. Flirtation had yielded to seduction, an outright manipulation of all that was tempting.

So what's the difference? Flirtation is breezy, fun, and in the moment. Seduction has an agenda; it is about the *future*. Anytime you meet a person with your agenda, then you, by definition, can't be in the moment. You are trying to manipulate a particular outcome that will happen in the future.

Aside from stealing you away from the moment, this can work against your happiness in many ways. You may be so focused on your agenda that you miss out on the rest of reality. In Frank's case, he so wanted to put Ashley in the "mine" box that he wasn't even paying attention to what she wanted. He couldn't hear what she was saying and see what she was doing, let alone know what she was feeling. It was all about him and what he was going to do for her and what they were going to do together. All this with a woman he had just met.

This is an exaggerated version of something we've all done, to some degree—planning our marriage to somebody while on the first date. Although it isn't always as extreme as in the story above, we all daydream a bit, wondering, *What if . . . ?*

When Ashley went to Europe with her ex, Frank was devastated. He honestly didn't know what he had done wrong. Hadn't he been generous? Fun?

Yes, he had. But he hadn't met the moment with innocence. He'd made the decision that he wanted Ashley. He'd reached into his available bag of tricks and pulled out money (other tricks might be sex, adventure, or family). And then he went for it. But ultimately he got hurt. He didn't see the situation clearly because he was focused only on where he wanted to go.

Does this mean we can't flirt and be sexy and spend money and crack jokes and do all the things that make the courtship process fun? Not at all. You can do all those things, but from a place of innocence and fun, rather than from a quid pro quo stance. Meet each moment with innocence instead of agenda. In this way you are awake, not merely seeing the world through the goggles of your own desire.

Frank felt that because Ashley had let him pay for everything and buy her gifts, she was his girlfriend. He didn't do it freely, with innocence, so he was hurt when it didn't go the way he wanted it to go.

So don't seduce. Instead, play. Don't desire it to go anywhere. Meet the other person without thinking about the future. Pay attention to the moment at hand; it will tell you everything you need to know.

The truth is, the only way you can get to the "future" you want is one moment at a time. It's impossible any other way. And by projecting into a future outcome, you actually miss out on the present moment, which, ironically, is the only time you can make that future happen—by your actions right now. So forget about the future. Be loose and free and yourself—swinging with what is happening. The correct outcome will naturally flow to you, whether or not it is the one you think you want.

The truth is that your great future, the one you dream about with all your heart, can only arrive as a result of what you do *now*, of how awake and loving you are *now*.

The deeper truth is that the future never comes; it only arrives as a series of eternal NOWs.

So bring it all down to right now, even as you read these words.

Now is the only moment that is real.

# MUTUALITY

## Fall into Your Tribe

If you judge people, you have no time to love them.

MOTHER TERESA

"I just love how masculine he is. How adventurous and well-traveled. He just lives life by his own rules, completely outside the box. Not like these clingy, New Age freaks who just want to talk about their feelings all day!" Kate gushed about her new boyfriend, who's a cinematographer for music videos and commercials. "He's like a dream."

"Uh-oh," I said, familiar with the symptoms, especially with Kate, who has a history of choosing dreams that turn into nightmares.

"Now, Arthur, don't be so negative! You're supposed to be spiritual and positive, not cynical about love."

"Who, me? Cynical?" I said. "There is a difference between being cynical, in which a person believes the worst in people, and being awake, which is seeing situations clearly."

"But you haven't even met him yet! You don't know him."

"I don't need to know him, I know you," I said. "And you're a homebody. You like to cook and have family and friends around. You hate to travel. You're also very loyal."

"Well, I have to be to put up with you, now, don't I?"

"You also love to analyze people and relationships. You *like* to talk over human motivations and feelings."

"Yeah, but I don't really want the guy I'm with to have more feelings than I do!"

We both laughed at the truth of the statement. Women are always complaining about men and how cut off they are from their feelings, but when it comes right down to it, women aren't that attracted to men who are more fluent than they are in the language of feelings—at least not initially. In the beginning, it's all about the fantasy of the masculine, strong, romantic man who's going to fulfill their fantasies of adventure and fun.

So Kate and George started dating, and it was the total fantasy. They flew to exotic places and had amazing vacations in between George's out-of-state stints as a cinematographer. And it was all great, especially the sex, which was infrequent, but wonderful when it happened.

But then his constant work, even when he made more than enough money, started to wear on Kate and the relationship. When she tried to engage him in conversation about it, about their relationship, he shut down. He completely lacked the tools to go deeper. It almost seemed as if they spoke different languages. He was also very flirtatious with other women, and over time Kate began to feel insecure, especially when his sex drive subsided.

Then one night she came home early to her apartment, where she was going to meet George (he had a key by this time). She entered the dark apartment and heard nothing. There was only a soft light from the bedroom.

"George?" she called. There was no answer.

She entered the bedroom and nobody was there. The bedding was rumpled and a light came from under the bathroom door. She opened the door and found George sitting on the toilet, leaning against the wall. A hypodermic syringe lay on the floor.

He wasn't dead. He had just nodded off after shooting up with heroin, something it turns out he had been doing on and off during the entire relationship. They were having problems as a couple, and now she discovered that he had a problem with heroin. He had lied to her all along, and many of the "work trips" were actually excuses to hole up in his apartment and get high. The lack of sexual desire wasn't due to an affair, it was the drugs.

Kate was suddenly faced with the decision of whether to leave or to stay with George, help him through his rehab, and work on their relationship.

"I don't know how much of our problems are his addiction and how much are our basic incompatibility," she said to me one day, in the throes of suffering. "I don't know what I should do. Should I stay in it and work on it?"

I stared at her. The issues were so deep. She needed to look at why she'd ended up with an addict, which meant her own twelve-step program. If she stayed with him and worked on it, it could take years. And this could be fine, a way for her to grow, a beautiful path of personal growth that many people take. But I felt that at the end of the day, even if they were both the best that each of them could be, they simply had inherently different values. They were different people, with very different ways of communicating.

"I can't answer that for you," I said. "What do you think?"

"I talked to my dad about it. Well, you know, he's my dad. So what's he going to say, right?"

"What did he say?"

"Well, he's a pilot, right."

I nodded. Her dad never was one to mince words.

"He said that helicopters can't fly with jets. He said I should find somebody who can fly with me."

"That's a great way to put it. How's that feel?"

"It feels pretty truthful. But I'm wondering if I'm just lacking the commitment to do the work."

"What about your commitment to yourself to be free and happy?"

She looked at me, nodding.

"But there's so much . . . potential here." Kate paused. "Arthur, what do you think?"

"I think potential is shit," I blurted out. We both laughed. "I mean, let me phrase this in a more 'spiritual' way. Potential is all about the future. Say you are living in hell right now with a person, and it just feels awful, that is the truth. Potential is the mind coming in and saying that in the future it could work out. Someday, over the rainbow. But in my experience, it doesn't. If it's not mostly working out right now, if it's not easy and with a certain kind of freedom right now, then chances are it won't work out in some mythical future. Especially in the first year, which is supposed to be the honeymoon period."

"The best indication of future behavior is past behavior?" Kate said.

"Exactly. People think partnering is about 'working on their relationship,' and at times that is true. Stuff comes up.

But it is the stuff of life. If the relationship is intrinsically mostly work when there are no external problems, then I would question it. Believe me, life itself serves up great dollops of suffering that will challenge your partnership. You don't need to create challenges yourself."

"This is so hard. I feel entwined. It's so painful to lose him."

"Yeah. It looks hard," I said. "But what is it that you're actually losing? He travels all the time. He wasn't communicative when he was with you. He was on drugs the whole time. What is it that you're really losing?"

"I'm losing . . . I don't know . . . him!"

"Or is it the *idea* of him? The dream of him, or of a relationship?" I challenged. "Again, isn't it the mind entering into the equation, dreaming about the future potential, regretting the past, and being anywhere but the present reality?"

"You are such a bastard!" But she was nodding her head.

Letting go of the dream of a person, of a way of life, is often as difficult as letting go of the person. The reality of a bad relationship is not very fun. But the dream of what it could be, well, that can be a huge attachment and usually has something to do with trying to fix our original wounds. We choose to be with some version of our mothers or fathers or siblings, attempting to heal the wounds created from that relationship. So when it doesn't work out with our partners, we have to not only let go of them, we have to let go of the *dynamic* that we are so used to. In a sense, we have to let go of the person who caused the original wound—or at least let go of the idea we can change them and get them to love us the way we think we should be loved. We have to let go of the original and childlike wishing for a dream of happiness. This is often what creates the deep sense of loss around the ending of an otherwise unhappy relationship, a partnership that we should even be glad is over. In fact, it isn't until the original wound is healed that we will end up choosing a different kind of person.

"Look," I said. "I've said too much already. But you asked. Do what you have to do; I'll support you either way. And either way will be fine. Truly. Maybe you need to go down the road a bit. Maybe it will work out. It doesn't matter—either way will be a growth experience. Either way will teach you about love."

Kate ended up staying with George for another year. It was up and down and back and forth, but they just couldn't seem to be together in a harmonious way. The mythic potential never panned out. One day she just woke up and saw them for what they were together. Incompatible.

Helicopters, with their own unique capabilities, still can't fly with jets.

# SELF-REVELATION

## Stop Hiding Out!

*There isn't any formula or method.*
*You learn to love by loving.*

ALDOUS HUXLEY

"I don't know, he's . . . kind of boring," my friend Patty was talking about a new guy she was dating.

"Boring? He's a journalist. He travels the world, going from one hot spot to another. How can he be boring?"

"Well . . . I don't know . . . he never reveals anything about himself. Nothing personal."

"What? Like where he went to school? What his favorite color is?" I still wasn't getting it.

"No. What he feels about things. What his take on life is."

"Oh, you mean he's one of those people who talk about *things* and *events,* rather than feelings and opinions."

"Yeah," Patty said. "In other words, he's a guy."

It was funny, but the inclination to reveal who you

are is not based on gender. I know plenty of women who have a hard time revealing anything about themselves, who are struck inarticulate at the very thought of venturing an opinion that might make them vulnerable to criticism or judgment.

The only time anybody is really boring is when they don't reveal themselves. I have friends who are brilliant, educated, articulate, and very self-revelatory. But they are no more interesting to me than another close friend who dropped out of high school and has never had an interesting job. They are interesting not because of what they know, not even because of who they are. They are interesting because they reveal themselves. Why is this interesting, in and of itself? It is interesting because every person is different, a unique universe of experience that you could spend a lifetime exploring.

There is no such thing as an uninteresting person.

Sure, you say, but you haven't met my uncle Frank, whose idea of an interesting conversation is to talk about the size of the tomatoes in his garden. But even somebody who is not talking about something that interests you can still be interesting. If you are curious about them, about what makes them tick, about what makes them passionate, then you can have an interesting conversation about anything, and you will often be surprised about where the conversation can go. All it takes is curiosity on your part, and their willingness to open themselves up. Curiosity equals presence and a lack of narcissism.

So why don't we all make ourselves interesting by revealing more of ourselves? Because we are afraid or shy or bored ourselves. Or we don't understand that most thoughts and emotions are universal; that if we are having a thought or feeling, chances are other people are having them as well, usually in the same room. This is called "voicing the collective consciousness," and some people are geniuses at it. They can just speak the thought that everybody is thinking, but didn't know it. Or knew it but were too intimidated to say it.

Thoughts and feelings are universal currency. In the realization of the dharma, the recognition is that it's all one blast of consciousness and we are all different manifestations of that consciousness. So how could it be any different? In this realization of our consciousness (or Godliness, if you prefer it), you realize that it's all consciousness having a conversation with itself: God seeing God through God's eyes; different aspects of the One. And how could that be boring?

This is where the nondual meets the personal.

Of course we all have our own histories and conditioning (both nature and nurture), that form our personalities: you are born into one family and you are a Muslim, you are born into another family and you are a Jew. In one you inherit or develop a sense of humor, in another musical ability. The simple truth is that your personality, the thing that you hold to be so dear, the thing that you won't reveal to anybody for fear of ridicule, is an accident of birth.

Ironically, as you start to lose your identification with your personality, as you stop taking your *identity* from your thoughts and emotions and work and hobbies, you stop taking yourself so seriously. As you lose this identification with your small self, you begin to not care so much about your personality. You just kind of let it rip! You know that it is not you. You drop the persona because you know that the consciousness from which it arises is the same for everybody.

To a certain degree, human beings are very fluid with

their personas. At work we reveal more of one persona, with a lover more of another, with parents yet another. Different aspects of personality are revealed for different circumstances. This is a normal, even necessary part of social adaptability. Without it, people act in ways that are seen as inappropriate.

But this is not what I'm talking about when I say "Drop your persona."

We all know what it is like to be with people who are quintessentially who they are, and are comfortable with that. It's easy to hang out with such people; they are easy to talk to because they are not hiding behind any kind of presentation. Their energy is high because they are not constraining their flow; they are not exhausted because they are holding a presentation together—they are not trying to be a certain way or project a certain image. They are easy in the world, able to swing with what is, because they are not trying to control their effect on other people.

The opposite occurs when you are trying to present an image and not reveal too much of yourself that might conflict with that image. For instance, if you are trying to be thought of as successful, you are attempting to control what other people think of you. So you won't let out any part of your humanity that might not be perfect. After a while this becomes exhausting.

Better to be free in the world, not identified with anything—not your thoughts or your feelings or your personality.

Then you let things out, you reveal yourself, and you can never, ever be boring.

# MONEY

## The Symbolic Symbol

I have no money, no resources, no hopes.
I am the happiest man alive.

HENRY MILLER

One of the most common causes of conflict in relationships is money; couples fight about money and sex more than anything else. The biologic imperative is alive and well, even in the twenty-first century. Men are chasing beautiful women (sex), and women are chasing powerful men (money) who can create a safe place for their children. This often results in clashes.

Both sexes make the basic mistake of identifying either sex or power as necessary for their happiness. At the core of this error is a kind of objectification that prevents us from actually seeing the other person in front of our eyes. How often do men look beyond physical beauty to see a woman's inner beauty? How often do women overlook a man's achievements to see what lies in his heart? How often have men, drawn by outer beauty, found out the hard way that the beautiful woman, after a lifetime of having doors open because of her beauty, hasn't developed an interesting intellect or personality? Or, even worse, has become a narcissist? And how often have women, drawn by a man's external success and power in the outside world, found out that they are actually insecure, overcompensating, and incapable of intimacy, workaholic and not available? But in spite of this, even some strong women have a deep-seated urge to find the man who's going to take care of it all—handle the storm if it comes.

We are all conditioned to follow a kind of false currency—beauty or power—and often learn the hard way that it is seeing each other clearly and with compassion that is most real and important.

So, how do we deal with our biological hardwiring, which is biased toward objectification? How do we become free?

The first step is to identify that we have been conditioned in the first place, whether through nature or nurture. This isn't to say that we ever lose this conditioning, especially the biological. But when it comes up, it doesn't completely swamp our screen of awareness. The biologically based desire gets triggered, but we take a deep breath and find some spaciousness around the desire. We notice other things. How kind are they? How do they treat the people around them? How are they in the world, loose and rolling with it, or tight and impatient? You keep the awareness that the conditioning, whether nature or nurture, is not who you really are. You are free of both, and all it takes is to remember this.

The second step is to realize that the core of this kind of

objectification is a kind of spiritual hunger, even when we don't know it. It is like a person who has a lot of sex without knowing that what he or she is looking for is love. We become overly identified with external definitions of self, belying an internal emptiness. Into this emptiness we pour possessions and experience, attempting to ameliorate our loneliness and separation. The less connected we are with our true selves, the less aware we are of our interior landscape, and the more we pile on either material possessions or other people to make us feel important and good about ourselves. Everyone knows the cliché of the balding, middle-aged guy with a twenty-three-year-old beauty as a symbol of his virility/success, and the beautiful girl using an older successful man who finds her desirable as a way of feeling good about herself.

There is no freedom in this, because the very process of trying to fill oneself up with external possessions or people leaves one feeling empty and lonelier than ever. There is also no real *friendship* in this way of relating. When the looks fade or the money disappears in an unexpected job loss, what is left? At the core of every successful relationship is the warmth and support of friendship—taking the other person as they are, without their so-called "currency."

Although there are plenty of opportunities to lose ourselves in the trance of identification, nowhere is it more prevalent than our relationship to material possessions and to other people and *their* material possessions.

So, in this context, what is money and how should we deal with it in our romantic life? Money is simply energy. This is not just metaphorical, it is literal. It takes energy to make money.

I have a good friend who is going out with an extremely

wealthy man; he showers her with gifts and jewelry and even gave her a car. But he is always working and doesn't spend any time with her.

"I really love him, but I don't know how much longer I can be with him," my friend complained one day. "I never see him."

"He certainly is generous," I said, sitting in the front seat of her Mercedes.

"Yes, but he's not generous in a meaningful way," she said. "The money means nothing to him. If a guy who has no money gives me a gift that costs money, then that is really generous. If you have a ton of something and then give some of it away, how generous is that?"

"But maybe this is the way he knows to be generous," I said.

"What would really be generous would be if he gave me his time."

And perhaps this is a definition of generosity: the giving of something that is precious to both the giver and the person receiving.

I once went out with a beautiful woman who was amazingly cheap. I paid for *everything*. Well after the courtship phase was over, she hadn't even bought one dinner or one movie ticket. There was disparity in our income at the time; I made more money, so I didn't expect her to be able to keep up. But I was thinking that at some point she would make a token offer, that she would give what she could. But it never happened. We broke up eventually—actually, she broke up with me—not because of money, but because the money became symbolic in our relationship. I was the caretaker and she was the receiver; the energy never went the other way, and the money was just an extension of the underlying emotional reality. She was not only parsimonious with the money she had, she was ungenerous with her emotional self, she wasn't disclosing or vulnerable or open. That, too, is a measure of generosity; how much of yourself are you willing to reveal? How much of yourself will you risk giving?

I have another friend who was married to a very wealthy man. He made a ton of money, but when it came time to give her a meaningful gift, on her birthday or on their anniversary, he invariably cheaped out. He bought the most inexpensive jewelry at the airport gift shop, or a truly hideous piece of clothing that didn't reflect his wife at all. It was almost as if his gifts were given as a form of contempt. They eventually divorced, not because of the money, but because of what the money represented. It was used in a way that didn't cherish his spouse and when she left him, it was because she realized he didn't see her clearly and, more important, didn't value her enough to try to see who she really was.

Money won't make or break a relationship; you don't need more than a middle-class income to be happy. In fact, studies have shown that the difference in happiness between the poor and those in the middle class is large. But the difference in happiness between those in the middle class and those who are very wealthy is nominal.

You can only be in one room at a time, drive one car at a time. You can only eat and drink so much. Be careful of the dynamic of greed, for once you are in its clutches, it is difficult to become free.

Money is only energy.

Don't let it be a tool for separation.

# AMBIVALENCE

## Always a Sure Thing

People in the West are always getting ready to live.

CHINESE PROVERB

About six years ago I met a woman at a dance class. Jecca was beautiful and danced like a dervish; we ended up dancing and spinning and laughing, finally collapsing on the floor in a puddle of sweat and desire. Of course I asked her out and she immediately said yes.

Three days later we sat across from each other at a restaurant in Malibu. Her black hair shone in the candlelight as we talked animatedly about life. There was a definite vibe between us, aided by a bottle of wine. We were having a great time and were in the thrill of discovery with each other. You know the part of meeting somebody where you don't see them clearly at all? Where you are living fully in the land of projection, of *projecting* who you think they are. I mean, I didn't know her at all, so the mind, in its inimitable way, was filling in the blanks.

Carl Jung said that the first six months of getting to know somebody are mostly projection. Think about it, the other person is a *tabula rasa* upon which we project our thoughts, feelings, and expectations because we don't know them. We see what we want to see, rather than what is. Then, as the person becomes more and more distinct to us, we start to take back those projections. *Oh, he really isn't generous,* or *Oh, she really doesn't like children or baseball or my laugh.* At the end of the process of taking back the projections, we are left with the real person, warts and all. At that point the real relationship begins or ends.

This isn't to say that people don't tell you who they are immediately, whether they want to or not. People are usually *screaming* who they are to you. But under the influence of a cocktail of infatuation, desire, and need, who pays attention to the little telltale signs? In an ego-based approach to love, we are seeing what we want to see. We are also getting high on the drug of infatuation.

So at this dinner I was months away from having any idea who was sitting across from me. Jecca looked at me with her deep brown eyes and said, "I've been waiting my whole life for somebody to look at me the way you look at me."

I simply stared at her.

"What do you mean?"

"Well . . ." Jecca smiled, slightly embarrassed. "You're so . . . *present.* You're so . . . *here.* You give me all your attention. It's intense. I like it. It's something I've been waiting for."

"Thank you," I said, genuinely touched. "That is the nicest thing to say."

"It's rare. It's a rare quality." Jecca scooped a large teaspoon of chocolate mousse and began slowly licking it off the spoon. "Most guys—they don't have a clue. All they think about is what they want."

Jecca licked the spoon again. Her tongue wasn't Mick Jagger large, but it wasn't that far off, either.

"Yeah," I said. "Well, I try not to have an agenda."

Jecca put the entire spoon in her mouth and sucked all the chocolate off.

"How's the mousse?" I asked.

"Fantastic!" She smiled at me, and we both had only one thing on our mind. We didn't go for it that night, but it was as obvious as the chocolate on Jecca's lip.

Our next date was a hike. All the way up the mountain, Jecca, wearing tight shorts and a belly-tee, waxed philosophical about our incredible connection.

"This is so *amazing!*" she said. "We have so much in common. I've been waiting my whole life to meet somebody who likes hiking in nature as much as I do."

"Really?" I said.

"Yes, most guys just like to go to the gym. But you're into yoga and hiking and—"

"Chocolate mousse," I said.

Jecca laughed a hearty laugh.

"Yes, let's not forget the chocolate mousse."

After the hike we went to my new apartment. I had just moved in, and everything was in boxes. I was on a deadline to finish two scripts for different studios, and my computer wasn't even set up yet. I said, "Listen, let me take a quick shower, then you can take one. We can grab a bite to eat. But then I've got to start unpacking."

"Okay."

"You want to go first?" I said.

"No, you go first, I'm going to play with Omar." Jecca picked up Omar, my beloved tabby cat. "I can't believe you like cats. I've been waiting my whole life for somebody who likes cats."

I stared at Jecca. *Hmmm* . . . was all I could think. Things that make you go *hmmm*.

"You've been waiting your whole life for a lot of things," I said.

"That's true." Jecca grinned.

I got in the shower. Three minutes later the shower door opened and Jecca came in, stark naked. She was slender, with fantastic curves.

"So much for waiting," I said.

"I don't want to wait." She grabbed the soap and began strategically sudsing me. We kissed and made love standing up in the shower.

Afterwards, we went out to dinner. Now we were fully in the sway of the three horsemen of Infatuation, Desire, and Projection.

"You are amazing," she said. "We are amazing together."

I couldn't disagree, yet there was something about her hyperbole that troubled me. It was too quick and easily earned. Long experience had told me that instant connection was usually a sign of some dysfunction and that the connection could be dissolved just as easily.

Two days later we went for another hike. I asked her what her plans were for the weekend.

"I've got a date tomorrow night with this guy I kind of like."

I stopped and stared at her.

"What?"

"Well, he's kind of cool. You know. I want to get to know him."

"Let me guess, you've been waiting your whole life to get to know him."

Jecca stared at me, a strange glint in her eye, as if she was enjoying what was going to come next, the way a fighter might look at a weaker opponent.

"Does this bother you?"

"Do you want to see other people after everything you've said this week?"

"I don't know. I think so."

"Really? Wow. Okay." I stared at her full lips as they curved into the smile of a woman who was used to winning her power struggles with men. She was that beautiful.

"That doesn't bother you?" she asked.

"Why would it? You can see whomever you want; I'm not going to be around for it."

The smile faded.

"What do you mean?"

"I mean that we're done. We are in different places. You and I will become friends."

"Okay. Fine."

She didn't really believe it. But I did. I had been down the road too many times of trying to make it work with somebody who was ambivalent or chronically had a "rain check" lined up just in case it didn't work out. If she really cared for me, she would close all her open doors. I knew the syndrome; I had *lived* the syndrome. If Jecca hadn't been so doe-eyed in her assertions of finally finding somebody with whom she was perfectly aligned, maybe I would have let it slide, maybe gone into competition for her affections. I'm sure this is what she expected and what propped up her ego——sending men into a feeding frenzy. But going from "You're amazing" to "I want to see somebody else while I see you," makes the decision pretty easy, even for me.

Ambivalence usually means no, for whatever reason. Forget about the words; if you really want to know what a person is doing, look at their actions. How many times have we been confused by a torrent of words that didn't add up to what the person was actually doing? When confused, watch the feet, not the lips.

Two months later Jecca came with a friend to a big birthday party I was throwing with my friend Charlie at a club we rented. We hadn't seen much of each other, although she had called me a couple of times. Still, we were cordial and I had sent her an invitation.

In the middle of the party, my friend Charlie came up, his face flushed from dancing and beer.

"Arthur, dude. Are you and Jecca completely finished? You don't have any interest in her at all?"

"Finished before we even started."

"So you wouldn't mind if I asked her out? Because she is so hot!" Charlie said. "And I think she's into me."

"Nope. Just consider yourself forewarned. You know the whole story I had with her."

Charlie nodded and plunged back onto the dance floor.

Two days later Jecca moved in with him. After a full year of almost complete misery, Jecca capped the relationship by sleeping with Charlie's new business partner. He was shattered by the experience.

I had dodged the bullet and it had slammed right into my friend's forehead. Why? Because I had accepted Jecca exactly where she was; I'd seen her exactly as the manipulative flatterer that she was. I'd watched her actions.

Even when people aren't being as direct as Jecca was with me, they are usually telling you exactly who they are, even when they are trying not to. All the signs are there; the end is in the beginning. And that's fine. People can live their lives any way they want. The question is whether you are willing to see it, accept it, and ask yourself if you want to get involved.

Often we are excited by ambivalence; we want to prove we are worthy, or we love the hunt and the chase and the seduction. This is especially true if our conditioning has taught us that we have to work for the love we receive; we have to be perfect or smart or beautiful, and so we might choose situations where we repeat that pattern. Ambivalence can be like waving a red cape in front of a bull for some people. But if you think about your romantic history, you'll see that most of the time, ambivalence ultimately means no.

Because love expresses itself as a positive and free. *Yes!*

# PATIENCE

## The Right Person at the Right Time

*You cannot look for this Spirit,*
*For it is doing the looking.*
*You cannot see this Spirit,*
*For it is doing the seeing.*
*You cannot find the spirit,*
*For it is doing the finding.*

KEN WILBUR

As we saw in the last chapter, if you meet somebody and sparks fly, but they are not ready for a relationship, then it is best to walk away. The right person at the wrong time is simply the wrong person.

But what happens when the pull is so overpowering, the connection so undeniable, that it can't be ignored? Where you can't wait to hear what will come out of their mouths and you can't wait to see them naked? You've never felt this way in your life—butterflies in the stomach and sweaty palms in their presence, feeling like you're being deprived of oxygen when they're gone.

And what if, worse than that, the other person is in another relationship?

What do you do?

There's no need to *do* anything, except be patient. You can still have a relationship with that person, but one that is appropriate to the situation. Build a meaningful friendship instead of playing the home wrecker. If it is meant to be, there is nothing you need to do except stay in touch. If it is not meant to be, there is nothing you can do to make it happen.

Brad met Sarah, a friend of mine, three years ago. He'd been married for a couple of years, and Sarah was engaged to be married to somebody else. There was an immediate attraction, more so on Brad's part than on Sarah's—she saw him as married, herself as engaged, end of story.

But for Brad it was the beginning of a long process. He had gradually begun to realize that he had made the wrong choice in his marriage. His wife just wasn't the person he'd thought she was. This wasn't her fault; it was his, if anybody's. But after meeting Sarah and becoming her friend, he realized the depth of feelings of which he was capable, feelings that he didn't have for his wife. But Sarah was engaged and he was married. What was he to do?

Brad wisely decided that he should seek counseling for his own marriage. He continued to see Sarah occasionally, but instead of declaring his feelings, he put the focus back into his own relationship. But no matter what he and his wife did, gradually the marriage began to dissolve. After a year, they separated.

Sarah, in the meantime, had been on a horrible roller-coaster with her fiancé, Kevin, which included a pregnancy and an abortion. Throughout it, Kevin's response ranged from emotionally unavailable to verbally abusive. Sarah began to realize that this man was not the man for her. He was inflexible and emotionally dense. He wasn't sure he wanted children, and she desperately wanted them. She felt guilty about the abortion, which she hadn't wanted to have. They were in a nightmare of bitter breakups, recriminations, and tearful reunions.

Brad, his marriage disintegrating, could do nothing but watch. Finally, after two years of back-and-forth drama, Sarah ended her relationship with Kevin. She was depressed and mourned it fully. Occasionally she and Brad would get together for lunch or see each other at a social function, but although Brad still had the same feelings he'd always had for Sarah, he kept them to himself. It wasn't time.

After a long period of celibacy, Sarah finally had sex with somebody with whom she'd had an affair several years before. David was a playboy and not suitable for a relationship, but they had met in Paris and one thing led to another and *voilà*—they had sex. David didn't even ejaculate inside her, but two weeks later Sarah found out she was pregnant again. They were both stunned. David was even less ready to have a child than Kevin had been. But this time Sarah, who was a successful clothing designer turning twenty-nine, decided she could not have another abortion. She decided to have the child herself, and informed David of that fact. He said she was on her own, and she was fine with that. Eventually he came around, saying he did want some involvement, but limited.

When Brad heard the news, he was devastated. His divorce had finally gone through, but the woman for whom he had carried a torch all these years was having another man's baby! What did it mean?

On Sarah's side, she was now a single mom, telling herself that she would never find a man who would accept her and her child.

Finally, one day Brad and Sarah were driving up the California coast after attending a birthday party. They were two friends in the car, talking about life and Sarah's beautiful baby girl. They were both single, and they had both undergone incredible journeys of pain and growth—including a horrible period of postpartum depression for Sarah. Although they had both gone through their separate struggles during the three years since they'd first met, even during the darkest periods Brad had never lost his feelings for her. He maintained his profound sense that they were destined to be together, in spite of their mutual unavailability.

On that sunny day, listening to Sarah talk about her life, her baby, and her struggles, Brad was filled with love for her. He felt that he could hold back his feelings no longer. And, ethically, he no longer had to. It was time to learn what she felt about him, but he was terrified at what her response would be. What if she didn't feel the same way?

He pulled the car to the side of the road and he leaned over and kissed Sarah and poured his heart out. He told her that his life had changed when he first saw her, that he had fallen in love and never fallen out. He asked her if she had any feelings for him beyond friendship. It turned out she did. They got married six months later and she's pregnant with her second child. In line with all her wishes and dreams, he has accepted her baby as his own, even to the point of wanting to adopt her. He is warm and communicative, completely the opposite of Kevin.

He is, quite simply, the right person. And he was wise enough to wait for the right time.

Often our minds will tell us when we meet somebody we like, when we have met our "soul mate," that the rules no longer apply. All bets are off and it's full speed ahead because we'll never get a chance to meet this person again.

But the rules always apply. If you meet your mate with integrity and kindness, no matter what the circumstances, then the door is always open. If you rush the situation, acting contrary to your integrity, then that is the way the relationship will eventually end.

Instead, be like Brad—patient and wise.

# PART THREE

# The Beginning

## The Agony!
## The Ecstasy!
## The In-Betweens!

# FALLING IN LOVE!

## When the Bomb Hits

What's love got to do with it?

TINA TURNER

What does it mean to fall in love?

I think we use the word "fall" because that is exactly what happens. We lose control and plummet into another person. Often it ends in a crash landing, after which we are wondering, *What the hell was that?*

And what exactly is the difference between infatuation and what I call true love?

Our society is completely geared up for infatuation. From *Romeo and Juliet* to our romantic comedies, love is ascribed to one glance, one fateful look, an immediate feeling of oneness with another person. But is it really love?

There are two aspects (at least) of love. One is love the *feeling,* and the other is love the *action.* Love the feeling is much like the intoxication one feels after taking drugs. It is a high, make no mistake about it, perhaps the most potent high in the world. For some people it is possible to get as addicted to the high of infatuation as other people do to the high of heroin, cocaine, or Ecstasy. Drugs and alcohol are *substance addictions.* The other kind of addiction is what is called *process addiction,* and it may be hidden in many different forms, including love, sex, gambling, shopping, work, etc.

So why am I talking about addictions when I talk about love?

Because I would say that infatuation without the second part of love, *love as an action,* is simply akin to a really good high. It is such a good high that some people can't get beyond it and spend a lifetime on the hunt for it. They get it, enjoy it, and, after it fades, move on. The pursuit is the end—there is no happily ever after.

We have all been on the receiving end of this dynamic of amazing connection and sex, followed by abrupt abandonment. I have been there often with the same person. I once had a girlfriend whom I saw on and off over the course of three years, during which she broke off the relationship repeatedly. Every three months, Carla would break up with me for some reason, all of which seemed perfectly natural at the time: she needed space to deal with some issue coming up with therapy, or she needed to move back home to sort out her relationship with her father. She would have to take a "time out" from us.

Invariably, just when I was getting her out of my system, Carla would call. We would see each other and the sparks would fly. There was an intense connection between us, both intellectual and physical; we would no sooner see each other than we would feel the need to be in each other's arms. It would literally take me about two minutes to completely forget how abruptly she had ended the previous relationship.

I was like Charlie Brown with Lucy and the football. In the *Peanuts* comic strip, Lucy promises Charlie Brown that she will hold the football in place so that he can kick it. And every time, just as Charlie Brown reaches the ball, she pulls it away and he lands on his ass. Every single time. No matter how much Charlie pleads, hesitates, or initially refuses to do it, he is eventually cajoled into it by Lucy, and the result is the same. It's in her very nature to pull the ball away. And Charlie, in his hopefulness to finally kick the ball, refuses to see that nature.

Once there was a scorpion at the edge of a river who wanted to cross to the other side. He looked around and saw a frog.

"Mr. Frog," said the scorpion, "won't you please give me a ride across the river on your back?"

"Why would I do that?" asked the frog. "You'll just sting me."

"But if I stung you, then we would both drown in the river," said the scorpion. "Why would I do that?"

The scorpion had a point. And so the frog let him climb on his back and they set out across the river. Halfway across, right in the middle of the river, the scorpion stung the frog right in the back.

"Why . . ." gasped the frog with his dying breath, as they were both drowning in the river. "Why would you do this to us?"

The scorpion shrugged (if scorpions could shrug), and said, "I'm a scorpion."

With that, the frog and the scorpion sank to their watery deaths.

Well, this is what it is like when you are in love the feeling; you can tend to ignore the nature of the person you are dealing with. Carla would always come back with her latest epiphany, and just like Charlie Brown, I would believe her because I so *wanted* to believe her, because I so wanted to get high on infatuation with her, that like any drug addict, I would ignore reality and would plunge right into our fantasy world. But she was a mirage that receded as I drew closer.

This lack of clear seeing will get you every time. And you can't expect the other person to act differently. This is who they are, no matter what they might be saying or wishing. They might actually want to act differently, to show up, to not sting you again, but it's not in their nature—they can't show up with *love in the form of action*.

It is very confusing when you fall in love. Overwhelming feelings appear. There is euphoria and chemical and biological change; vows are exchanged, words like "love" and "forever" and "one-of-a-kind" are bandied about. There isn't very much to do because there is so much *feeling* happening.

But as you are inundated with feelings and words, don't ignore actions, for they are much more likely to tell you what is really going on. Often the mind gets involved here, telling you what you *should* be doing.

"He's so good-looking, who cares if he treats the waiter like dirt." (I want him, so I will ignore his character.)

"She's so sexy, who cares that she flirts with every man she meets?" (I want to have sex with her, so I will ignore her neediness.)

"He's famous, so what if he pushed me further than I was comfortable." (I want to feel better about myself by being with somebody famous, so I will ignore his objectification of me.)

Notice that in each of these circumstances, desire of some sort has obscured clear seeing. This is understandable. But if the guy is saying, "You're so amazing, I love you, I want to be with you forever," but is not being consistent, not calling you when he said he would, standing you up on a regular basis, then trust the actions, not the words.

When the love bomb falls, the first casualty is often our ability to see clearly.

So what are we supposed to do? Give up on the romance and excitement? Not follow our emotions? Nah. What fun would that be?

Desire will hit, sparks will fly. And who wants to miss out on that?

Just let the desire arise, but keep some awareness around it. Keep a little spaciousness around it so it doesn't completely fill your screen of awareness.

Know that you have taken a hit of a very powerful drug. Enjoy the ride. But it isn't true love. It's a drug trip that may or may not lead to true love.

# THE END IS IN THE BEGINNING

## So Tell the Truth Faster

*A flower falls, even though we love it;*
*And a weed grows, even though we do not love it.*

DOGEN

Molly met Jake and fell in love with him almost immediately. Jake was a "healer," and she had attended one of his workshops. He was charismatic, rich, handsome, and spiritual, all qualities that Molly found attractive. He said he was separated from his wife and three children, and he invited her to come with him on one of his programs in the Australian Outback, using the healing techniques of the Aborigines. It was literally their first date, and fulfilled all of her expectations of romance and adventure. She had finally waited long enough, and here was her real-life spiritual Indiana Jones. Jake traveled the world over, and Molly loved the travel and the excitement of it all.

During that trip, many of Jake's students treated Molly like she was only the latest in a long line of conquests. They didn't take her seriously, and assumed that she was just a fling. She heard rumors that Jake was a womanizer and that he hadn't separated from his wife until after Molly met him. But because they all put Jake up on a pedestal, Molly thought this was just jealous cattiness.

The trip was a smashing success, and Molly and Jake began a relationship. For the first two years it was fantastic; they moved in together and began plans to build a house.

For those two years they met in exotic places where Jake was teaching, or he came to California to be with her on his off time, of which there wasn't a lot. He was always flying off somewhere, and seemed restless when he wasn't working. Over time, Molly saw that Jake had no other intimate relationships or friendships. He had a toxic relationship with his ex-wife, and barely saw his three children. Jake was often cool and distant, using his work to hide from being with her. He was, in spite of making a lot of money, cheap with Molly—hoarding his millions and never treating them like a team.

The things that Molly valued the most—intimacy, family, generosity, and hanging out with friends—were things that Jake couldn't care less about. After a while she realized that they had nothing in common. He was only interested in work, and his work started to seem questionable to her. How was passing a feather across the body of a terminally ill patient and then charging him hundreds of dollars actually helpful? Or ethical? She had a conversation with Jake's

ex-wife, who confirmed that they were not actually separated when Molly started to see Jake.

Another way in which Jake and Molly were incompatible
was that she enjoyed an "open system" relationship, one that
was filled with friends and family and entertaining. Jake was
only interested in her, creating a stifling and closed system.

Molly and Jake ended their relationship after five years,
amid bitter acrimony. By her own admission, she stayed in
it three years too long.

"What happened?" Molly asked me one day. "How did I
end up with this person? What did I do to deserve this? I'm
a good person."

"This happens to all of us," I said. "Don't beat yourself
up, but it's worth asking the questions 'Why did I choose
this?' and 'Was there a sign right at the beginning?' "

A long silence.

"I guess it was there. I just didn't want to see it," Molly
said. "It was all so romantic and fun."

THE END IS IN the beginning. People are usually screaming out who they really are right from the start; they are
not leaving bread crumbs along their trail, either; they
are usually leaving whole loaves of bread. Small things are
usually indicative of larger things, and when you look at the
little things, you can usually extrapolate out into the bigger
issues.

So pay attention. Be awake.

What good is the dharma, if it is not going to prevent
you from choosing unnecessary suffering? What is the point
of internal freedom, if you can't see the human bullets coming your way? It is like the scene in the first *Matrix* movie,
where the bullet is coming at Keanu Reeves and he simply

leans back, letting it go by him. This doesn't mean you have to be fearful or cynical or suspicious. It simply means that you are awake and that your sight is not obscured by your desire.

In fact, you can tell just about everything you need to know on your first date by observing how your date treats the waitperson. Does he flirt? Is she impatient? Does he treat service personnel like dirt? Does she feel entitled? Does he tip appropriately? Is she polite?

The end is in the beginning.

When I met Jake, he couldn't look me in the eye. He seemed uneasy with himself. He was restless and never revealed anything about himself. When we were alone, he would try to bond by making jokes about women, what a hassle they were, how you couldn't live with them, couldn't shoot them. I could see his discomfort with intimacy because I wasn't involved with him; when I am involved and in love, my sight isn't as clear. But I could see Jake, no problem. Later in the relationship, my friendship with Molly became an issue for him. Instead of looking inward at his intimacy issues, he looked outward at the mostly easy friendship Molly and I had, saying that it was the reason his relationship with her wasn't working. But for many years Molly was completely devoted to Jake. When he was in town, she would disappear off the radar, ignoring her other friends.

She even went so far as to make the mistake of trying to change Jake, trying to get him to slow down the pace of travel. Each year he would promise to cut the travel down from 80 percent to 50 percent. Each year nothing would change. He was a rolling stone; it was what he was most comfortable with. She stayed in the relationship for years longer than she thought she should have, trying to make it work.

And Molly shouldn't have been surprised. He was exactly who he seemed to be on their very first meeting, he didn't change at all. She just didn't want to see it, nor did she want to give up her romantic illusions about what love should look like.

We all do this. I have fallen madly in love twice in my life. Both times the people fitted my ideal in terms of chemistry, looks, and intelligence. Both times they were unavailable for real relationship, unable to commit, or didn't share my values. And this information was staring me in the face right from the beginning. Did this stop me from pulling out all the stops and going for it?

Nope.

Will any of this information stop you? Probably not.

Still, when the siren call of love reaches your heart, know that the rocks that might sink your happy boat are usually right there in plain sight.

Waking up means seeing and acknowledging them.

And let's say that you do fall madly in love with the wrong person. Don't beat yourself up. It happens. But don't stay in it years longer than you should, telling yourself some story. We all do this, and the stories are as varied as we are:

She's the only one.

I'm too old to start over.

I can't support myself.

I'll never recover from this loss.

I'll never find another like her.

I'll never love again.

As the story comes up, recognize it is a product of the

mind. Do not sell out your happiness in the present moment for any mythical future. As the Buddha said, "There is no way to happiness, happiness is the way."

Do not believe the thoughts that are arising. They are not you.

If you see the truth about a person, just see it, without the story.

Take a deep breath and proceed, moment by moment, with your life.

Even if that means walking away.

# SURRENDER AND ACCEPTANCE

## Can't Love Without It

Commitment is inherent in any genuinely loving relationship. Anyone who is truly concerned for the spiritual growth of another knows, consciously or instinctively, that he or she can significantly foster that growth only through a relationship of constancy.

M. SCOTT PECK

The essence of love is surrender.

It is the main ingredient involved in making a decision to be with somebody. You know that moment—and it is a specific moment—when you say to yourself about another person "You're it." There is a sense of closure, almost a sense of relief. It is a surrendering to trust and commitment, the two cornerstones of intimacy.

We spend so much time and have so many choices in modern life. But studies have shown that the more choices we have, the less happy we actually are. When people have fewer choices, they are actually less neurotic.

There is frantic anxiety up to the point of making a decision, but then calm comes after making it. Many people report this sequence on the days leading up to a proposal or marriage. High anxiety, then relief.

This may sound funny, but the same process happened with my beloved cat, Omar. Taking on a pet is a lifelong commitment—not for everybody, perhaps, but for me it definitely is. When I was growing up, my family had a dog that lived until he was sixteen and a cat that lived until he was nineteen; the cat was actually older than I was by a year. They were members of our family.

So, when I decided to get a cat, it was no small thing. I took it seriously. I started looking at kittens, going to different animal rescue facilities and the pound. I stared deep into the eyes of hundreds of kittens, waiting for that magical moment of recognition—love at first sight. I know, it sounds hilarious, but it was a function of my own desire to be able to make a commitment that I could keep, to surrender a part of my life to this hypothetical kitten. How often do we have the same attitude toward finding a mate? We don't increase our ability to love; instead we search for the perfect person.

But I had a hard time finding the right kitten (don't we all?). I had an idea of what it should look like, I knew what its "vibe" should be—not neurotic, because there's nothing worse than a neurotic cat who might pee in your bed when he gets mad at you. And I was certain I wanted a kitten, since I didn't want to inherit any problems from a previous owner. And the kitten definitely could not be as neurotic as I was being in my search.

One day when I went to the grocery store, a pet rescue facility had set up an adoption center outside—dogs and cats in cages—so I walked over. And that's when I saw Omar, a twenty-pound tabby with fluorescent green eyes and an attitude. He was unhappy, but in a very distinct way, as if he was bearing up under all the stupidity of humans.

"He's been in the cage for three months," the woman who worked the adoption center said. "He was abandoned and was living in some backyards in his old neighborhood."

She opened the cage and pulled Omar out. His head was the size of a cantaloupe, and his neck was thick with muscle, but his vibe was big and lovable. I sat there for two hours, agonizing over whether I should adopt him. He wasn't a kitten; he had had a hard time, and who knew what kind of problems would come from the trauma of being abandoned? Still, even in his unhappiness, he was an amazing cat, the kind of cat I wanted my kitten to grow up to be.

"It's so hard to adopt out full-grown cats," the woman said. "Everybody wants kittens."

"I'll take him." I said. "Will you hold him while I go get a cat box and food and get them set up at my house?"

"Of course," she said, smiling. "You won't regret this."

As I drove off to a pet store, I found myself overcome with emotion. It was like something had broken in me, just by making the commitment. When I took Omar home, I put him in the covered cat box so he would know where to go. He sat in there for an hour, he was so used to being in a cage. When I pulled him out, he crawled under the couch and wouldn't come out. I lay on the floor and stared at him: he was fluffed up, sitting on his white paws, which were touching each other. His green eyes looked worried.

"Come on, Omar. Come on out," I said. "It's okay."

Omar didn't budge. I tried tuna fish, I tried reaching for him, but nothing made him move. So I just lay on the floor for a couple of hours, looking at him, occasionally calling out to him.

"It's okay, Omar. You're okay now," I said.

Then he inched toward me.

"That's right, Omar. Come on out."

He looked at me and made a decision. He scurried out from under the couch and into my arms. I picked him up and scratched behind his ears.

And we haven't been apart since.

What is it about pets? They give their unconditional love and trust to us, and we, in turn, give it to them. We think we are rescuing a dog or cat, but in reality they are rescuing us. They help us love.

The basis of this is commitment.

There will always be moments when having a dog or a cat will be work. They get sick or they need to be walked at 7:00 a.m. on a freezing cold morning.

The same is true of being with a partner. Sometimes it will simply be work. There will be days when you won't want to do it. You remember the freedom of being single, and sometimes being with your partner is a drag, no matter how great it is overall. There will be sickness or conflict or full-on fighting.

But it is through the commitment that we weather those storms.

And it is through surrender that the commitment is realized. You are not simply surrendering to the other person. It's deeper than that. You are surrendering to the fact that you don't have any control when you love somebody else, because other people are essentially uncontrollable. So you surrender your tight control of your little life, you trade it in for the messiness of other people. You allow yourself to become vulnerable.

Omar has never peed on my bed—in fact, he's never peed anywhere but the cat box (except for one time when I emptied his cat box into a plastic bag and he peed on that because he got confused). But this doesn't mean he won't. Someday he will get old and might need a lot of help. It's inevitable every time you love, but that's okay.

Some people feel incomplete unless they are in a relationship, as if something is missing. They are lonely. But many of us are fine by ourselves. I have a lot of friends and family, and my life is very peaceful when I'm single. I have gotten to the point in my life where I don't want to be in a relationship unless it is a real addition; I would rather enjoy my peace, freedom, and internal spaciousness, for which I wouldn't trade anything.

But there is aridness in being single—nobody gets in your face, so you can cruise for a long time without growing. There are ways of being challenged in a romantic relationship that just don't come up when you are single.

Because love involves surrender, it necessitates making yourself vulnerable to the vicissitudes of another personality. And at some point, no matter whom you are with, that personality is going to cause you pain because nobody is perfect. You are letting go of your expectation of perfection, both in yourself and your partner. So you are also surrendering to the fact that at some point your beloved will cause you pain. This is a scary thing to do.

But take comfort that the clear and present awareness upon which both personalities arise is untouched. So to surrender one's ego is okay. To lose one's identification with the small self, the story of me, what I want and when I want it, is an actual freedom.

You accept and surrender to it all, even the cat that might eventually pee in your bed.

# STDs

## Not the End of the World

*Life is a sexually transmitted disease.*

R. D. LAING

One in four adults has herpes (approximately thirty million Americans).

There are approximately one million new cases of genital warts each year.

Chlamydia is a rapidly growing sexually transmitted disease, with almost a million new cases a year.

The possibility of HIV infection hangs over every sexual experience with a new person. Sex can literally equal a lifelong disease or death.

Depending upon who you are and what your experience is with sexually transmitted diseases, these statistics will have different levels of a chilling effect. What is the best way to navigate romantic relationships and sex in a world so fraught with disease? Obviously all diseases aren't the same, but have different levels of symptoms and seriousness.

My friend Greg has herpes. He's had it for years and hasn't had an outbreak in a couple of years.

"How do you deal with it?" I asked him. "I mean, it's not like you're contagious all the time, so do you have the difficult conversation right from the start with potential lovers?"

"I have to," he said. "I explain the risks, let them make their own decision, and I use a condom after they do."

"I had a girlfriend who had herpes," I said. "She was incredibly responsible, patiently explaining all about it, being very conservative about her exposure to me. I never got it."

"Yeah," Greg said. "That's the way to go. Most of the time people get it from people who don't know they have it—it can sit dormant for years. But I got it from somebody who knew and was just irresponsible. That really sucked."

"Why didn't she tell you?"

"She said she felt ashamed. She thought I would leave once I found out." Greg's eyes narrowed. "I was so pissed off that I left after I confronted her."

There's a sense of shame attached to STDs that other sufferers of disease don't have to deal with. Ironically, this sense of shame, this story that somehow "I'm a bad person" because I got this disease having sex, actually promulgates the disease.

"I really hated having herpes," Greg said. "I still do. But in a weird way it works out okay. It separates people out who aren't serious. It also prevents me from being a dog and going after every girl I'm attracted to, because I have to sit there and think, 'Is this worth the trouble of telling her this embarrassing thing about myself?' "

"Are you still embarrassed?"

"No, not really. It's just something I live with. It's a part of who I am. But still, it's not an easy talk to have with a stranger."

I think this conversation is instructional on many levels. It shows how to be truthful with other people about the condition. It initially seems like a huge deal, filled with embarrassment and dread, until it finally becomes something you live with. Everybody with whom I've spoken who has herpes has told me that the disease itself isn't that bad: an outbreak once or twice a year, with sometimes none. And what does an outbreak entail? According to people who have it, only an uncomfortable burning sensation that lasts a few days to a week.

The suffering, like so much of life, comes from the mind telling itself a story: the "shame" story, or the "this shouldn't be happening to me because I'm a good person" story.

But it has already happened. There's no point in picking an argument with reality—that never works and is just a waste of your precious life. As far as feeling ashamed goes, it's understandable given our cultural squeamishness around the human body. But if you had any other kind of condition—if you broke your leg, for example—you wouldn't waste a moment feeling shame. You might get engaged in another kind of story, depending upon how you broke it, but shame probably wouldn't be part of it.

The point is, the mind is the source of much of our suffering as we go through life. There is pain or discomfort, in this case from the symptoms resulting in sores. But the rest of the suffering is extra.

Greg has arrived at an incredible way to look at his condition, actually finding in it a positive side. The condition prevents him from jumping too quickly into meaningless sexual encounters, helping him to act more responsibly by giving him a moment of pause to judge his emotions and the connection he really feels. It gives him the opportunity to tell a difficult truth to a woman whom he just met and in whom he is interested. And it acts as a litmus test for his potential partners, demonstrating to him their level of maturity and interest in him.

So even something as unpleasant as herpes can act as a call for wakefulness.

The dharma posits the idea that *everything is one thing*. It all appears to be different, yet is actually the same, namely consciousness or awareness. All of it is happening without our planning or even doing anything. Like fruit growing from a tree, we are all part of the one blast of consciousness that animates all, even though we may feel like an individual piece of fruit. Everything, even a sexually transmitted disease, is part of this consciousness or awareness.

The thing that separates us from this realization is the mind. The mind is constantly breaking things into "good" or "bad." The mind makes distinctions and separations between things it likes and dislikes. It is always concerned with the little "me." Obviously it's going to jump all over the negative aspects of an STD like herpes. But once you stop identifying with the thoughts produced by the mind, then you begin to experience simply *what is*. And at the end of the day, it usually isn't so bad. You are dealing with some unpleasant symptoms, not the end of the world. And even if it is more severe, even if it is AIDS, then the same awareness applies. You will have symptoms; you might even have painful symptoms. But don't add to that pain by adding the story of shame, or "I'm going to die," or anything else. We don't know what the future will bring. I know someone who has been HIV positive for seventeen years and is healthy.

So, instead of creating separation with an STD condition, you create connection. You use it to become more authentic, more honest, and more communicative. Like everything in life, it becomes a way to grow.

# JEALOUSY

## The Green-Eyed Monster

Jealousy is not a barometer by which
the depth of love can be read. It merely records
the degree of the lover's insecurity.

MARGARET MEAD

One night, about a month after we met, my new girlfriend, Alice, took me to a cowboy bar on Sunset Boulevard in Los Angeles. The bar was packed with boisterous patrons, cheering on the braver (or drunker) people getting tossed from the mechanical bull. I don't usually drink and I rarely hang out in bars, but I was thoroughly enjoying the spectacle, thinking about what an imagination consciousness has.

Into that scene waddled an enormously fat man carrying an umbrella (it wasn't raining) and a wad of hundred-dollar bills as thick as my fist. Accompanying him was a slender young Asian man wearing an expensive suit and carrying a briefcase. The fat man—he must have been three hundred pounds—came right up to us and looked at Alice's drink and waved down the bartender with a couple of the bills. We made room for him.

"What are those?" he wheezed, pointing at Alice's drink.

"It's a Cosmopolitan," Alice said.

"Pretty color," he said. "Gimme . . . twenty of those. For the bar. On me."

He gave the bartender two hundred dollars and told him to keep the change.

The man introduced himself as Howard. His sidekick was George, fresh out of Stanford with an MBA. Howard lived in Hong Kong and said he was psychic. He was in L.A. setting up an all-psychic cable station. He claimed to have helped the FBI solve many missing-persons cases. He was genial, kept the drinks flowing, and was absolutely un-like anybody I'd ever met. Not because he was psychic— I saw no demonstration of those abilities, and indeed I have no idea what he actually did—but because he handed out hundred-dollar bills to everybody who did anything for him. Bring him a drink, a hundred dollars. Wipe the bar in front of us, a hundred dollars. Pretty soon we were in the middle of a feeding frenzy of good service and hangers-on, scooping up the free drinks that kept coming. But for some reason he stuck close to Alice and me.

"This place is too predictable," Howard said after an hour and too many drinks to count. "Where can we go to see some ladies? Any good strip joints around here?"

"There's Crazy Girls on La Brea," Alice piped up. "It's a good place."

"Crazy Girls. Now that's a good name for a strip joint. Honest advertising," Howard said. "Let's go."

Alice finished her fourth Cosmopolitan and looked at

me with a look of sheer carnality. I shrugged, just finishing my second drink, which for me, with my daily yoga practice, is the equivalent of five drinks for most other people. Why not? Howard certainly was one of the more interesting chips of consciousness floating around the planet.

"Okay," Alice said. "We'll come."

Howard settled the tab, which was over a thousand dollars. I wasn't sure what his thing was; maybe he had his eye on Alice, maybe he just wanted to have a good time. My instinct was he was lonely and trying to fill himself up with more. A man of obviously gargantuan desires, he needed excessive stimulation to feel anything. But my other feeling was that he knew Alice and I were kind people who didn't really want anything from him. The night was taking an unexpected turn, which is always fine with me. It certainly beat the movie we'd planned to see.

So off we went to Crazy Girls in Howard's rented Cadillac, with George driving. When we entered the strip club, Howard gave each of the bouncers at the door a hundred-dollar bill.

"We need a table," Howard said.

We were immediately ushered to a banquette. Howard ordered Cristal champagne and handed out hundred-dollar bills to every stripper and waitress who approached. By the time we sat down, we were surrounded by ten girls offering us lap dances. He probably spent two thousand dollars on that walk. I saw George open the briefcase and take out another stack of hundreds. It was like play money.

Dancers gyrated on the stage, all of them uniformly unoriginal in their G-strings and fake breasts. I'd been to a few strip clubs, usually with bachelor parties or with girlfriends who were curious, and Crazy Girls was anything but crazy. It was less Moulin Rouge than sports bar. Still, it was packed, there was lots of action going on, the music was loud, and it felt like a party.

As I looked at Howard negotiating a lap dance and George pouring champagne for Alice, and the suitcase on the table, and the girls onstage dancing to David Bowie's "Golden Years," and the bouncers subduing a drunk patron, and the disco lights bouncing it all around the room, I became very still. I disappeared as it all washed over me and I merged with all I saw. I became the girls onstage, the rowdy drunk, the shimmering disco ball. It was all consciousness, all God, playing itself out in its infinite imagination: the dancer's high-heeled shoe, the pole she was draped around, the beer spilled on the floor, the dollar bills tucked into the dancer's G-string, all of it pulsing with consciousness, including the "me" that had disappeared.

I found myself grinning. How amazing to have this direct experience in the middle of a loud strip club and not on a silent retreat; to sense the spiritual that infused everything, the lack of separation that came from a lack of judgment.

The universe tilted and whirled in that club. It was vibrating with energy and infused with God and I vanished. Even the dance the strippers were doing began to feel like part of some ancient atavistic ritual, a pagan homage to the sacred feminine.

"Arthur! I see a lap dance in your future," Howard said, leaning over to me, his big face sweating from the exertion of chatting up strippers.

"Is that a proper use of your psychic abilities?" I joked. Howard laughed so hard the sweat fell off him like water off a wet dog. I'd never had a lap dance. Not from lack of opportunity, but more from a lack of desire. It seemed like too short a step to prostitution.

"Yes!" Alice jumped up, feeling no pain. "And I want to watch."

"Are you sure?" I asked. Alice grinned and nodded.

"Pick one," Howard said expansively, as if talking about a necktie. And so I did. She was the only dancer who seemed to enjoy herself while dancing, who seemed to like teasing and toying with the men. Her breasts were real, or at least not cartoonishly fake. She wore cut-off Levi's hot pants, which gave her a whole sort of seventies, Daisy Mae thing that worked. She smiled like she had just won the lottery when I pointed at her.

"I'm Chantal," she said, taking my hand and leading me into one of the private rooms. Alice was on my other arm. Okay, I thought, this is uncharted territory. Chantal sat me down and Alice sat opposite me, across the small room.

"She's watching?" Chantal glanced at Alice. "Okay, what ever works for you lovebirds."

"Every person has their sexual lock and key," I mumbled, drunk. "I say, nothing to do but try to be accommodating."

With that piece of sodden wisdom, Chantal hit the music (Love to love ya, baby) and started to rub herself all over me. I could smell her perfume and the slightly acrid odor of her sweat. She turned around and gyrated her ass in my lap.

"You like that, big boy?" Chantal moaned. "You like that?"

I nodded, it was a caricature of eroticism, but the truth was I was not stimulated at all. I was watching Alice's face and seeing something that I didn't expect. She was upset. She suddenly looked furious and sad at the same time. The dance suddenly felt about as erotic as watching somebody washing my car, it was that impersonal. Chantal took off her halter top and shook her breasts in my face. I could smell the talcum powder and waited for it to end.

The song ended and Chantal stood up, turning off the carnality like a faucet.

"You want another?" she asked. "Maybe the deluxe would work for you. The fat guy said for me to stay as long as you wanted—get you a little more into it."

"No . . . um . . . that was great. Really. You're an artist."

Chantal shrugged and walked out. I went over to Alice.

"You okay?"

"Fine."

But she wasn't fine. She was upset and sad all at once. She was jealous of the stripper and had feelings for me that were only now surfacing. And it was completely irrational. I wasn't going to do anything with the stripper. I wasn't even interested in the stripper, and the whole thing about Alice watching had been her own idea. But jealousy isn't rational. And it certainly isn't love. It comes from fear of losing the object that we think is supplying us with love. It is the fear of an addict who might lose his drug. It comes from not knowing that the love we feel is ours. And it is completely human; we have all felt it at one time or another.

When this fear comes up, it is best to simply notice it and trace back to the thought that preceded it. There is always a thought before the feeling of jealousy, even if it comes up because your partner is acting in a way that is flirtatious or inappropriate and jealousy might seem to be a natural response. Trace back to the original thought, whether it's "he shouldn't be doing that" or "I'm not good enough to keep her." Examine whether the thought is true.

Or is the deeper truth that your partner is simply insecure and acting out on it? Is the deeper truth that they are not the source of your love? Because this is the truth: *You are the source of your love, which is part of an infinite connection with the universe.* It cannot be taken away by another, it can only be given away by you yourself.

But don't beat yourself up for feeling jealous. Just notice it as another conditioned thought and come into the NOW moment. Allow it to be your portal out of the quagmire of your thoughts. And even if jealousy is arising in the NOW moment, don't go for the ride. Understand that all the suffering is based on the wrong assumption that somebody else controls whether or not you are able to give and receive love.

Take a deep breath in that moment and just let it all go. Go to the "worst case" scenario and imagine yourself single. Let the relationship go, let go of control, let go of any identification with thoughts. Notice how it's as simple as not identifying with the thought that *this shouldn't be happening.* It *is* happening, but you were fine before you met this person and you will be fine after they are gone. You are not in control of another person's behavior; as soon as you realize that, you are free.

And if you see that your partner is jealous, try to have compassion. They are suffering, so don't pour gasoline on the fire. But if they are irrationally jealous and controlling, if they cross the line into wanting to know where you are, what you're doing, whom you're with, know that there is very little you can do to change their behavior. Their fear is such that they will be relentless in their attempts to control your movements and behavior.

There is another aspect of this: just as a thief only sees

thievery, expecting the worst from people, a jealous person only sees adultery, a projection of their own inclination toward infidelity. So be awake when your partner is accusing you of cheating, of being jealous, of looking at other people. Sometimes it is simply insecurity, but often it is a projection of their lack of fidelity. Either way, like a python slowly wrapping itself around its victim until its prey can't move, somebody with this level of fear will eventually squeeze the life out of a relationship, and perhaps out of you, too.

But in the very human garden-variety jealousies that come up, the best response to their fear is compassion.

"Let's go home," I said to Alice. "You can give me a real lap dance."

"Home? No way." Alice sounded furious. "Howard wants to go to the Pussycat after hours. No alcohol, but the girls get all the way naked."

"Fine, but I can assure you that it's going to get depressing."

"I'm fine. You just didn't have to enjoy it that much."

"Believe me, I didn't." I kissed her and she brightened. We went out to the main club and the lights were coming up. Howard was negotiating with some of the girls to come out and party with us. They all promised to, but outside in the parking lot, after waiting for twenty minutes, Howard realized they weren't coming.

"If ya can't trust the word of a stripper, then who can you trust?" he said laughing, his Texas accent slurred. "Onward to the Pussycat."

And so we went. And it was depressing. The energy was not titillating; it left nothing to the imagination. The customers seemed lonely or drunk or angry—or a combination of all three. The bouncers were surly, and the strippers working the room were strung out and pushy, circling the men like vultures, feeding on their loneliness.

I wanted to leave right away, but a quick glance at Alice, who was dancing with one of the strippers by our table, told me that she wasn't ready. I relaxed my awareness. What was the point of wakefulness if it could only be summoned when the picture was frothy or rosy or buzzy or beautiful?

Consciousness has an imagination. Consciousness plays rough. Consciousness has created everything in the universe, and lots of it is the unending dance of creation and destruction. It's so easy to put people in the "other" category, to create separation. But there is no "other," there's just consciousness, amusing itself in infinite ways.

In Crazy Girls I was able to drop my identification with my mind and feel connected and at one. In this bar, I was judging and categorizing everything I saw. But it was all human, and humane. My judgment was a function of my mind.

Nothing human is alien to me. Is this not all just one taste? My revulsion, my lust, my confusion, the bouncer's bicep, are these not all contained in the ever-present awareness that holds the entire display?

Perhaps you are wondering what kind of spiritual book this is, taking field trips to strip clubs. To paraphrase Ken Wilbur in an essay on "sages": Do you want your teachers bloodless? Dead from the neck down? "Transcending" the difficulties of sex, money, food, relationships?

If I avoid these difficulties, does that mean you get to avoid them, too? You won't have to embrace life with gusto, with all its complexities and verve. We can label something "bad" and just sit back with a gentle smile on our lips and not have to deal with the messy, unsightly aspects of being human. "Egoless sages," who are above all that is messy, juicy, complex, pulsating, desiring, and urging forces, are what people want. To quote Wilbur directly: "Religion, they believe, will simply get rid of all baser instincts, drives and relationships, and hence they look to religion, not for advice on how to live life with enthusiasm, but on how to avoid it, repress it, deny it, escape it."

We can repress it all, label it as "immoral" or "bad," slam it in a box and throw away the key. Or, better yet, let somebody else sit back with the spiritual smile, somebody to whom we can hand over the responsibility for our spiritual life, while we do whatever we want.

But this book is about the dharma. And the core teaching of the dharma is that there is no separation. That's just an illusion of mind. It's all God. In the nondualistic teachings there is no shame, guilt, or story about sexual desire—it is a part of life. There is no separation of the body from the "soul," just as there is no separation from ourselves and God. The body and soul are inseparable, as are God and ourselves—they are one.

The guilt and shame that have been handed down through our patriarchal lineage has done a lot of damage to the way we treat sex and love and our bodies. We are embodied creatures, and the more we embrace the body and celebrate it, the more we are connected to life. So drop any conditioned story or judgment about your body's desires. They are natural or they wouldn't exist in the first place.

This is not to say we don't keep an eye on a distortion of natural desire. I mean, it was being used and exploited in that club. But the more I relaxed in that "sleazy" strip club, the more I was able to drop into love. Was not the man throwing money at the stripper the Self waving at me, another part of the Self? Was not the entire bar one blast of God or consciousness or Atman or whatever culturally conditioned name we have given the great mystery, self unto self, love unto love?

That lasted ten minutes, and then I was suddenly tired. I said to Alice that I was ready to call it a night. And we did, after a long good-bye to Howard and George.

After we stumbled into her apartment, Alice told me to wait a minute. She emerged ten minutes later in thigh-high black latex boots with high heels, and a miniskirt that barely covered her ass. A bikini top rounded out this picture.

"That lap dancer, she sucked," Alice giggled, putting on Sade.

And compared with Alice, she did. We easily fell into the nondualistic state that sex provides. The moment for orgasm, or *la petit mort,* "the little death," as the French appropriately call it, is a powerful way in which the little self dies for a moment.

Obviously orgasm has a lot going for it; mostly it just feels incredible. But one of the unmentioned aspects of orgasm is the point where the "I" disappears into the "we," the dual becomes nondual. "You" get to disappear. It is for many people their only taste of total wakefulness, the only time they are not self-referencing, their only release from the bondage of "me." I'm convinced that aside from all the physical delights and the expression of love, one of the main pleasures of lovemaking is this taste of freedom from the small self, freedom from the thinking mind.

When you begin to look at life through the paradigm of wakefulness, you begin to let go of your opinions of what is "good" or "bad." If it is all one blast of consciousness, then what could be "bad"? Instead you begin to look at the world as a part of yourself. The angry person, the jealous person, the needy person, indeed everybody you encounter, becomes another manifestation of consciousness, a part of the whole. And each of these "persons" is within us. We have the capacity for every kind of behavior, given different circumstances.

So, when jealousy arises, either in you or in your partner, don't judge it. See it, follow it back to the thought, and try to keep some awareness around it. If it is unprovoked, look at it as a kind of short-lived madness. If it is provoked, take a deep breath and try to look at it as an opportunity to grow and communicate with your partner, who may be acting out. A cry for love and attention can take many forms, and either provoking or feeling jealousy is usually a symptom of fear. Recognize it as such, and work with it.

Don't deny your shadow and pretend it doesn't exist. For if you do, that green-eyed monster will surely come back and bite you in the ass! Instead, embrace it—have compassion and a sense of humor about your darker side. In this way you will tame it without banishing it to the basement, where it can lurk and cause all kinds of mischief.

Make friends with your shadow; for it is you.

# ANGER

## Let the Sparks Fly?

The angry people are those people
who are most afraid.

DR. ROBERT ANTHONY

I have a friend who has a problem with anger. He doesn't think so, but he is the most easily irritated person I know. He reacts to almost everything with irritation and a sense of judgment.

"You always know where you stand with me," he says, in his Russian accent. "I don't mince my words like you Americans, always trying to be politically correct."

The problem with this is that Peter is always reacting to circumstances in his life, and his relationships suffer.

"Would you rather be right or happy?" I ask him one day after he has complained that he had a fight with his long-suffering girlfriend. He furrows his brow for a moment, thinking it over.

"I would rather be right," he says. "The truth is the most important thing in the world."

"But you are always so irritated by everything. It seems as though no one can say anything around you without your getting irritated."

"That's the stupidest thing I ever heard!" Peter's voice rose in irritation.

"See what I mean?" I said. "What just happened here?" Peter laughed suddenly.

"Well, people are irritating. They don't know how to be in the world. They are always saying stupid things."

"Like me?" I said.

"Especially you," Peter said, laughing.

There are many theories on the best way to deal with anger. There was a time when anger was encouraged as a way of "letting it all out." You didn't want to keep things bottled up. Then later research showed that the more often you got angry, the more often you were likely to get angry. The more you react with irritation, the more you are clearing the neural pathways in the brain for this kind of reaction, resulting in a downward spiral. In short, regularly getting angry makes you angrier, even if it is conditioned thought that triggers the angry reaction and not what is actually happening in the moment. For Peter, his conditioned thought was "The whole world is idiotic and wrong and I must make it right."

Then, just to further add to the confusion, many forms of spirituality shy away from expressions of anger. It's a "bad" emotion.

So what is the best way to deal with anger when it arises?

First of all, anger is simply an emotion that arises and needs to be honored like any other emotion. It is not "wrong." It is not "right." It just is. There are plenty of circumstances in which anger is justified and is a motivating force to instigate necessary change. Swallowing one's anger in order to seem more "spiritual" does nobody any good— especially the one in denial about their anger—and it will lead to illness, both physical and mental. So an honest expression of your anger is necessary. Just don't let it completely swamp your screen of awareness.

But just like any other emotion that comes up, make sure the anger is happening in the moment. Make sure that the emotion of anger is in reaction to something happening in the here and now, rather than some story of what happened in the past. This ensures it is an authentic emotion.

In this way, too, you can feel it fully and then let it blast through. Anger arises, anger is felt and expressed, anger disappears. In this awareness it is best to express it directly, in the moment. Even though many teachings would advise you to wait to express your anger, if you wait, you are in another moment. And you have dragged the anger into that moment. You have dragged the past into the present, where it is preventing you from waking up. It's better to express it immediately with an "I feel" statement and then not hang on to it. Let it go.

After that, understand that a person in anger, whether it is you or somebody else, is in a form of suffering. Peter, in his way of being in the world, is actually suffering a lot more than the people around him, with whom he is constantly getting irritated. Thich Nhat Han, the Vietnamese

Buddhist monk, talks about what he does when anger arises.

"Please help me, I am suffering. I have anger," he says to people with whom he is angry.

Now, this might be a bit too much for you. But understand this truth: If you are the one getting angry at another person's behavior, *you are the one who has the problem, not they*. They are just fine, living life in the best (and perhaps only) way they know. They are just being quintessentially who they are.

This is sometimes difficult to grasp. But it goes back to my question of whether you would rather be right or happy. People cruise through their lives, a product of their particular conditioning. They are as indifferent as the weather to what you want. So their actions, for your own peace of mind, should be treated as impersonally as the weather. You wouldn't expect the weather to act in a different way than it does, would you? Much of the time we can see this; however, we lose sight of it the most when we are in a relationship of our own. We want to change the other person. We develop expectations of the way they should act. We learn how to say "you make me feel" instead of the more accurate and honest "I feel." "They make us mad," we might say. No . . . *you make yourself mad*. You are responsible for your feelings, not anybody else.

If there is one thing that can reduce irritation, anger, and difficulties within relationship, it is to reduce expectation of how your partner should act. They are going to be who they are. This is why you are with them in the first place. So Peter's girlfriend who reacts to his reactivity, who is volatile to his volatility, is just as controlling as he is.

Again, anytime you try to control another person—

how they feel, what they think, who they are—you are building a cage for them, but even more so for yourself.

And as far as anger goes, understand that it is better not to say the thing that can't be unsaid. Once it is said, it stays and lingers, and like a bit of toxic waste it can fester in the heart of the other person for years. So express your anger directly, but impersonally: "I am angry," versus "You are a complete asshole!"

This is not to say you must be perfect, for everybody occasionally says things they regret. This is not the end of the world, as it gives each person the ability to apologize and practice forgiveness. And sometimes this proves to each person in the relationship that they are strong enough to withstand the absolute worst that can come out of each other's minds. It proves that each party is willing to stay in the room when the going gets tough. This builds trust, a good thing.

And maybe this is where all relationships end up. Over the years, every last bit of decorum and politeness gets stripped away, every last ugliness is revealed, until we are totally naked with each other. But then every last ugliness gets forgiven; it is a beautiful thing. But beware of a habit-forming dynamic with your partners. We have all seen couples who can only communicate with each other by bickering; it can become a way of being so entrenched that it becomes invisible to us.

This is the point of dealing with anger. It arises. Don't deny it, but don't let it take over your screen of awareness as well. Express it directly in the moment with "I feel angry" statements, especially if it is not a part of some story you are telling yourself. Anger is only effective as a tool for change if it is happening in the moment. And remember that there is no such thing as an invalid emotion. Emotions aren't invalid or valid, they just are.

Anger isn't invalid or valid. It just is.

Forgive it in yourself, for it is natural.

Forgive it in others, for it is natural.

# FULL-ON
# FIGHTING

## No Kicking Below the Belt

As discussed in the preceding chapter, often those of us who are on a spiritual path find conflict difficult to deal with.

"I hate fighting," my friend Donald said to me one day. "It literally makes me feel sick to my stomach. My girl-friend grew up in a family where fighting was the normal way of communicating. I try to avoid it at all costs, but then when I do fight, I overreact."

"So you're a smolderer," I said.

"What?"

"There are different types of fighters. On the one hand is the 'mad bomber' who gets angry easily and expresses it, but with little control. At the other end of the spectrum is the 'smolderer,' who stores up complaints but doesn't ex-press them directly. Instead, 'smolderers' may seethe in-wardly and act out angry feelings in passive ways."

"Yeah," Donald laughed. "I guess I am a smolderer."

How about you? Do you ever use extreme or irrational tactics to gain your point (slamming doors, stomping around)? Do you sometimes hurt your spouse in order to have the last word (sarcasm, name-calling)? Do you store up grudges and use them to "hit" your partner at a later time (revenge)? Is your attitude "If I don't get what I want, I will quit cooperating"? Do you continually expect others to do things the "right way" (i.e., your way)?

If you answered yes to any of the above, you are *not* "fighting fair," and are creating an interaction pattern of "I win, you lose." If you continue this over time, you will be setting into motion a hurtful, destructive method of responding to differences and resolving disagreements, one that you may not escape.

Most couples fight about something, but many seem to differ about virtually everything and anything—which TV program to watch, where to go on vacation, how to discipline the children, how to spend money, who is going to work, what kinds of chores each has to do, and so on. Disagreement and conflict are part of the daily lives of many couples because marriage provides a fertile ground in which the seeds of conflict can germinate.

But conflict is a normal, inevitable, and even healthy aspect of most relationships. When managed well, it can be used to enhance and strengthen relationships with friends, family members, co-workers, and romantic partners. Fair fighting provides the tools and techniques to help you achieve positive results when problems arise.

So how do you do this? When ignored or unresolved differences pile up, so do irritations and resentments. Studies have shown that the small but steady irritation actually creates more stress than the huge catastrophe. When something big happens, people have a tendency to mobilize all their energies to deal with it, but they simply ignore the smaller stressor until it blows up. How well a marriage is working depends in part on how well a couple learns the skills they can use to negotiate and resolve their differences, and how satisfactorily they can close the emotional distance that has been created.

When a vicious circle of conflict dominates a relationship, each person feels angry, hurt, misunderstood, and rejected. Neither is able to trust the other. When this occurs, the couple has developed a "ritual impasse," in which they typically become stuck at the same point in every effort to make decisions and solve problems. The "stuck" husband, for example, might always block any conciliation attempt by predictably refusing to talk about it or being too tired after work. This effectively destroys the problem-solving process between husband and wife, and an impasse occurs.

If a couple is to move away from the temporary solutions of disengagement—of pouting and withdrawing or fighting and making up—to something more constructive and intimacy-producing, they need to agree to some rules and learn some negotiating skills. If not, there will just be an endless repetition of old wars that lead to "marital battle fatigue"! Remember, mature couples can be in control of the arguments rather than the other way around.

There are many books on mediation and fighting, and they all seem to break it down into roughly the same steps.

## MODEL FOR RESOLVING CONFLICTS IN MARRIAGE

1. *Recognize conflict issues.* No one has to look for conflicts, but if a disagreement arises, accept it as an opportunity

to gain understanding of yourself and the other person. Consider it a time of growth. Your pessimism or optimism toward the problem issue will influence conflict resolution.

2. *Listen carefully to the other person.* Any changes desired by either spouse have to be heard and understood. If you listen to each other, you will soon notice that you begin to take each other seriously.

3. *Select the most appropriate time.* It is very important to select a time that will allow for the greatest understanding and cooperative effort. If you are hungry, physically exhausted, emotionally upset, or have a limited time before an appointment, real problem-solving should be postponed.

4. *Specifically define the problem or conflict issue.* Look for the relationship between the problem as you see it and the underlying basic psychological need from which it might have arisen. How does each of you define the problem? In your opinion, what behaviors contribute to the conflict? What behaviors do you think the other person sees as contributing to the conflict? What are the issues of agreement and disagreement in this conflict?

5. *Identify your own contributions to the problem.* In resolving marital conflict, you are basically saying to another person that "we" have a problem. When you accept some responsibility for the problem, your partner perceives a willingness to cooperate and will probably be much more open to the discussion. Restate the problem to make sure you have correctly understood your partner.

**6. *Identify alternate solutions.*** Once each of you has identified your own contributions to a problem or conflict, it becomes clear that a behavioral change would be to everyone's advantage. The next step—the solution to the problem—is not always clear, however. Now is the time for individual and joint *brainstorming*. Each should think of as many solutions to the problem as possible. These should be behavioral changes both for yourself and for the other person.

**7. *Decide on a mutually acceptable solution.*** After identifying all of the alternatives, evaluate them and make a choice. Your evaluation of each alternative should include (1) the steps in implementation, and (2) the possible outcomes. What will be required for each person to effect a change by implementing a given alternative? How will the change affect the behavior of both individuals and their relationship? If one spouse likes a certain solution but the other finds it unacceptable, discuss the reasons. Mutual sharing can promote growth and prevent feelings of rejection on the part of the one who suggested the alternative. Continue until you agree to try one solution to see if it works.

**8. *Implement new behaviors.*** Concentrate on your own behavior changes and allow your spouse to do the same. After you have made the behavior changes mutually agreed upon, evaluate their effect on your relationship.

Another guideline I think is effective is the triple-win approach. When a conflict arises, you don't try to pulverize your partner and "win" the argument, for how many times have you won the battle but lost the war? If you "win" and your partner loses, how does this make them feel, and how does it damage the relationship? In a win-win situation, you are both trying to come to a solution that feels good to both. But in a triple-win, you are also taking the relationship into consideration; this is the third entity you are trying to protect and serve.

For example, say a couple is fighting about money. Jack wants Jill to take fewer classes per semester and get a job, so he can quit the night job that he hates, while Jill wants to continue her accelerated school program. A possible solution might be to move in with Jill's parents, who have offered to let them do it. Now, this might be a win for Jill (she can continue on in school) and a win for Jack (he can quit his job), but is it good for the relationship? Jill's parents are overbearing and controlling; they would be meddling in every part of their marriage. It is not a triple-win situation. When negotiating conciliation, all things must be taken into consideration, especially the relationship.

While there are tools and skills to be gained for handling conflict, remember one important truth: *Your partner is there for your spiritual growth.* And growth is sometimes uncomfortable; in fact, by definition it means traveling outside your comfort zone. It means at times you will be triggered by your partner's behavior or, quite bluntly, by their mere existence. Keep in mind at all times, even as you utilize active listening and negotiating skills, that non-identification with your ego is key.

When you stop identifying with your ego, "you" disappear. You go from "me" to "we" and "mine" to "ours." You realize that you are having a conflict with another chip of consciousness, the flip side of the same cosmic coin. *And that coin is you.*

So, no matter how intense a fight may get, don't put the other person out of your heart. For if you put them in a box of "wrong" or "hateful," you also put yourself in a box (right or judgmental). And from within these boxes it is impossible to communicate, never mind come to agreement.

# THERAPY

## If the Bone Is Broken, Go to a Doctor!

Life shrinks or expands in
proportion to one's courage.

ANAÏS NIN

"I've finally started to go through some major changes," my good friend Charlie announced one day. Charlie, whom I've known for seven years, changes his passions and personas at least once a year, each time with the all-in commitment of a marine jumping out of an airplane. When we first met, he was a budding commercial producer with Hollywood aspirations. He used to wear preppy outfits and tortoiseshell glasses. Then he got sick of Hollywood and wanted to become a Raw Food impresario. He tattooed Om on his chest, ate only uncooked food, and started a raw-food company. It didn't pan out. Now he wants to become a real estate magnate and has swapped out his Prius for a pickup truck and started lifting weights instead of going to yoga classes.

I love Charlie. He is like all of us, trying to find out what will make for a meaningful life with meaningful work, trying on different personas and figuring out what will fit. Along the way I've encouraged him at various times, especially after the breakup of a particularly bad relationship, or as a result of repeating patterns, to seek a therapist. He's steadfastly refused, preferring to see healers or go on drug-induced guided "journeys" as a way to understand himself. So I was a bit surprised at his announcement.

"Yeah, I just had to figure some stuff out. I'm seeing a spiritual counselor and also a life coach."

"Is she a therapist?"

"Oh no. She doesn't come from that paradigm. It's more a more spiritual approach."

He then went on to tell me that they were getting deeply into his parents' divorce and how that affected him—his relationship to his emotions, and emotion in general.

"But it isn't therapy," he assured me. "It's a spiritual approach."

I just smiled to myself. What he was doing was pure therapy. No doubt the woman had experience in counseling, but what she was doing was using a language that he could access. When you are talking about how things that happened in your childhood are affecting your present life, you are firmly in the arena of therapy.

Many people on a spiritual path are drawn to it out of suffering. They are looking for an answer to the pain they are feeling from a dysfunctional family, a divorce, alcoholism, or abuse. And so they head into spirituality, which gives them relief from the madness of their mind and the constant drip of their anxiety. Most spiritual programs teach them some practice to transcend their emotions, whether it is through meditation or chanting. Or they are introduced to the concept that they are not their thoughts, or are told to "drop their story," as in the teachings of this book. In short, painful emotions and thoughts are transcended. But are they really gone? Or have the techniques simply masked the symptoms, but not dealt with the underlying causes?

This is a difficult question to answer, and there may not be a single answer for everybody. But my own direct experience in working with myself and others indicates that if there was some specific past trauma that is causing the pain, or if there is some present trauma, often a therapeutic approach is helpful because many times we don't even know what it was that happened to us; it is repressed. And even in the teachings of this book, you can't really drop your story until you can first identify and understand it. So therapy is one of the ways in which we can understand ourselves, become awake to the forces that shaped us, and become able to see clearly the patterns that have emerged as a result of those forces, many of which are very specific and unconscious.

Which gets back to the idea of "if the bone is broken, set it." There is no other way to deal with certain problems. You can chant, you can pray, you can meditate, and all of it may help, but if some aspect of the personality is wounded in a specific way, then to not see it, feel it, and grieve it doesn't make for spiritual wakefulness but for a form of denial. And what a great kind of denial it is, because you get to be "spiritual" as well as avoiding doing some real work around the source of the pain.

I am not advocating therapy instead of a spiritual path, for all therapy ends in a cul-de-sac, with nowhere to go. You can only rummage around in the bones of your past for so long; eventually the story *must be dropped*. But there is no reason that therapy can't be an integral part of a spiritual path. In fact cognitive therapy is very similar to the teaching of this book: it's not what happens to you, it's your mind's relationship to what happens. Develop a different kind of relationship with your thoughts, and your suffering disappears.

If the deepest aspect of a spiritual path is to "know thyself," then all the different healing modalities can come into play. It is also important to know that as powerful as the dharma is, it isn't a panacea for all suffering.

There was a time during my dharma talks when a person suffering from paranoia came on a regular basis. He was a sincere man, deeply committed to the dharma. He was also convinced that people were stalking him for something he had done thirty years ago.

"You don't know, Arthur." David was intense, his face in anguish as he cornered me after a dharma talk. "I misbehaved, and everywhere I go, there are people watching me."

"But, David, this was thirty years ago," I said, after hearing it for the tenth time. "It seems far-fetched that they would even recognize you, never mind follow you."

"You've got to believe me!" David's voice was shaky.

I looked in his troubled eyes, trying to connect with him. "I need to ask you a personal question. Is that okay?"

David nodded fearfully.

"Have you ever been on medication?"

"Yes," David sighed. "I was on medication, but I don't like the way it makes me feel."

"I'll tell you what. I don't know what is true here. I can't speak to what your reality is." I tried to reach him in his deep suffering. "It may be true that people are following you—the world is a mysterious place. But why not try an experiment? Go back on your medication and see if you still believe you're being followed. Then you'll know. Will you give that a try?"

David looked at me and slowly nodded his head; he could see the sense of it. I didn't see him for a long time after that; he stopped coming to the dharma talks. But then I saw him on the street and we stopped and spoke.

"How are you, David?" I asked.

"Better. Thank you." He just looked at me. He didn't say anything, and neither did I. But we both knew why he was feeling better.

We are all broken. It is part of being human. And in no other place than in a love relationship will all those broken buttons be pushed. If you grew up in an alcoholic family and have the disease of perfectionism, then chances are being in a relationship is going to be difficult. So why not avail yourself of the best tools to make it work?

Self-knowledge can come in many packages.

And while the dharma advocates that you stop identifying with the thoughts that are surely a part of your conditioning, that you drop the story of who you think you are, it doesn't exclude other modalities. In fact, it's all part of the one blast of consciousness, whether it's therapy or whether it's medication to balance out the chemicals in a dysfunctioning brain. And thank God we have the science to do it. So don't label one thing "spiritual" and another "not spiritual." It's all spiritual.

And couples therapy can be invaluable. It can give couples tools to increase communication, break the deadlock of power struggles, and understand old patterns as they relate to one's partner. It can also expand on the commitment to stay in the room when things get difficult, for in a long and serious relationship, at some point things will get difficult.

So, without judgment, avail yourself of all the tools out there.

Anything short of that may not be self-knowledge, it might be denial.

# NTR

## "Not This Relationship"

Enlightenment is intimacy with all things.

JACK KORNFIELD

One of the main characteristics of being asleep, not awake to the present moment, is to be living in the past. Day-dreaming, wishing things were as they once were, or pining away for another person all rob you of the only livable moment that exists: *this moment right now.*

There is a Sanskrit word, *moksha,* which means liberation. What does real liberation mean? It means seeing through *maya,* illusion. Seeing through illusion is integral to, if not synonymous with, waking up.

I'm not using the word *illusion* as in "it's all illusion, so nothing matters." This is an immature and erroneous interpretation of the teaching. The world of our senses can be trusted. When you bang your hand on a brick wall, even though it is made up of rapidly moving molecules, it is solid enough to break your arm. The physical world has a certain reality to it.

So, what is the illusion to which the ancient mystics were referring? The world of *maya* that takes place in our minds is illusion. Our thoughts about what has happened to us in the past or what might happen to us in the future are illusion. Our interpretation of events is illusion, usually based on conditioning. Our identification with thoughts is illusion.

In short, the world of the mind is illusion.

We are not what we think. And in order to become liberated, to experience *moksha,* we must see this to be true. We must stop identifying with every thought that gets generated in our heads. Most of these are merely habitual; you thought them yesterday and you will think them tomorrow.

In relationship, this often happens as we consciously and unconsciously compare our previous relationship or experience with the present one.

My friend Ethan called me recently to ask my advice. Four years ago he had been in a very intense relationship with a woman named Jane. When they met, they were inseparable and she immediately moved in with him. And so began two years of hell. Jane was insanely jealous. She gradually began alienating Ethan's friends, unable to let him lead his own life and unable to lead hers. At some point in the relationship, Ethan actually came to me and sat me down.

His fingers drummed the table as he took a deep breath and began talking rapidly. "Jane and I think you don't feel our relationship can work. And I want you to know that this relationship is very important to me. If you can't be there for me, for us, then we can't be friends."

Now, Ethan and I had been friends for years. Over the past months he had told me bloodcurdling stories of Jane's tantrums and her flirtations with other men. His relationship was nonstop drama, and Ethan looked exhausted. He had also gradually cut back on the time he spent with friends and family, further isolating him. Jane had even asked him to get rid of Walter, his pet parrot, which he had had since he was sixteen. She thought he spent too much time taking care of the bird!

So this was not a healthy relationship. We talked for quite a while, and I said to him what I had always said, that I just wanted him to be happy, that a good relationship should make you a better person, that it was fun and a cause for celebration, rather than a nonstop working out of "issues." Not that issues don't arise, but they aren't intrinsic to the relationship itself. Life will provide plenty of external drama, conflict, and sorrow; a relationship with no external challenges should run smoothly more often than not.

But, most important, Ethan's relationship didn't seem to be making him happy. Ethan left that day feeling unsatisfied, saying that he just wanted support for the relationship. Nothing I could say or do would change that.

A month later Jane moved out, "needing some space." A week later she was involved with another man whom Ethan knew because he had a business relationship with him. Two weeks later she moved in with this man. Ethan really went through the wringer in that relationship, and four years later he still didn't have another girlfriend. He just didn't want to take the risk.

Ethan hibernated until he met Kim, an energetic and capable woman who had her own job and apartment. They started going out, and there was chemistry and a mutual interest in taking it further. Everything seemed to be going great until, two weeks into the relationship, Ethan called me.

"We broke up," he announced.

"Broke up? I didn't even know you guys had already reached boyfriend/girlfriend status. What happened?"

"I don't want to deal with the drama," Ethan sighed.

"What drama? I thought she was cool."

Ethan then told me a story about how Kim wanted them to get an HIV test, just to be sure. When Ethan didn't see the need for it, she got upset, feeling that he wasn't concerned with her well-being.

"She had a good point, I mean . . . she was *right*." Ethan sighed again. "But I just can't deal with the level of emotion."

"What was the level? Did she scream or . . . I don't know . . . get abusive and throw things? Was she unreasonable?"

"No. She just . . . I guess she just . . . was upset."

"But rightfully so, by your own admission."

"I don't want to deal with it. So I broke it off."

"But Ethan . . . Do you expect her not to have any emotions?" I groped around for a way to reach him. "You've got a case of NTR."

"What?"

"NTR. Not This Relationship. Every conflict with Jane resulted in a screaming match or stuff getting thrown or her storming out or kissing another man at a party."

"Yeah. So?"

"That was then, this is now. You're reacting to this relationship as if you were a shell-shocked soldier. You're not present to what's happening in this relationship, you're still dodging bullets from the last relationship."

Silence.

"You're right. I just don't want to be hurt again."

"But your challenge now is to open your heart again," I said. "You might get hurt. No, in fact *you will get hurt*. Because even if you and Kim end up getting married and growing old together, one of you will probably die first."

"Gee, you really know how to cheer a guy up."

"Anytime," I said.

We talked for a long time and Ethan decided to go back to Kim and explain what had happened to him and how he wanted to give their relationship a real chance. They are still together.

The business of being human is enduring loss. It all ends in loss and heartbreak, and nobody escapes it. We have the smaller but still devastating losses that come from dissolving relationships. And then we have the finality of separation from death. Life is, as the Buddha said, suffering.

But there is a way out of the suffering in the present moment. In Ethan's case it was as simple as recognizing that his reactions were not based on what was happening right now, but on what had happened in the past. His impulse to break it off with Kim after the slightest display of emotion came from the two years of craziness in his relationship with Jane.

Much of our conditioning is like that. A painful experience becomes embedded in our psyche, and when anything similar comes up, it gets triggered, causing us to overreact, like using a chainsaw to cut butter. The only way out of this is to become more present in the moment. In this way you have a chance of seeing reality clearly.

But how does one "drop the story" in the midst of a triggered response?

One of the ways is to watch our response to what is happening. Often it isn't what is actually happening that is causing us suffering, it is our *interpretation of what is happening.* Like Ethan, we have a conditioned response based on our past, so our interpretation of the present isn't clear. It is seen through the goggles of painful experience, distorting the NOW into "then."

But how do you combat this? As mentioned, one of the ways is to become as present as possible in each moment. It is difficult for the past to really live in the present moment because the NOW is too intense, too vibrant. Your thoughts and story about the past fade in comparison.

This process of seeing through your interpretation can also be helped by asking some simple questions. In Ethan's case, he could have asked if it was true that Kim was creating drama. And if she was, he could have asked if it was true that "he couldn't deal with the drama." Or if neither was true, he could have asked how he would feel if he didn't believe this to be true. How would this change his experience of life?

Taking a moment and asking yourself if your interpretation of reality is correct often provides a moment, in the *present moment,* to pause and recognize when you are not present, but simply running a past story.

There are many conscious and unconscious ways in which our minds deprive ourselves of the present moment. One of the most insidious of these occurs when we compare past

partners with present ones. But most of the time the relationship that really matters is the one you had with your
parents. Or the one your parents had with each other,
which was a model for you as you grew up.

We all learned how to love from watching our parents;
we learned our definition of what love is from the fighting
or abuse or alcoholism or passive aggression or true love.
There are as many different definitions of love between
parents as there are people on the planet. Much of it was
ego-based and not true love. But seeing your parents as
human and making peace with the way they loved you and
loved each other is important, even if it was very painful.

Understand: *Your parents did the best they could with what
they had.* They did the best they could, given the fundamental tools they were given from their parents. *And so does
everybody.* If you remember this, you will, as Paramahansa
Yogananda said, "have no expectations and therefore never
be disappointed." If you forgive your parents for their mistakes, you will be less likely to try to rectify their mistakes
in your current relationship by choosing the wrong person
and trying to fix *them.*

Nobody sees himself as the bad guy; we're all doing the
best we can. We may even see ourselves as the hero in our
own particular movie.

But there is no need to create that dynamic again for
yourself. If you suffered as a child, don't keep re-wounding
yourself as an adult. Don't keep telling the same story, over
and over, about what happened. Or do, with the realization
that at the end of all the work or healing or therapy or
alienation, you will finally have to drop the story to be free
of it.

When you are in an NTR moment, it is not simply "not this relationship." It is also "not this moment."

And it is "not this life," for your present life keeps getting stolen, moment by moment, as you drag around the baggage of your past.

# GENEROSITY

## Not Giving to Get

Although gold dust is precious, when it
gets in your eyes, it obstructs your vision.

HSI-TANG

"I'm a giver," my friend Shelly said to me one day. "But I always get involved with people who don't give back. They
never reciprocate."

"Do you expect them to?" I asked.

"Yes. I mean, why should I always be the one giving?"

It's a good question when you are in a relationship with
another person. Usually there is one person who is giving
more and one person is taking more. Often it is the women
who give more, but I don't find this necessarily indicative
of who the people really are. How many times have you
been in a relationship where you have been the giver, more
generous with your time and money, more of a caretaker of
the other person's emotional and physical life, more pres-

ent to their needs? Then, in the very next relationship, you become more of a narcissist, you become the person who is doted upon and around whom the relationship orbits.

And so goes the Ping-Pong effect of the giving game.

But what is the true nature of generosity? Was Shelly right? When you give, should you expect something back? Is love a barter?

This is one of the trickiest subjects in a spiritual approach to relationship. The deepest truth is that love is expressed through generosity. But what if you give too much—can you get burnt out and resentful?

Well, yes and no.

Yes, only when you expect something in return. If you are giving, and expect something in return, is it really a gift given freely from your own heart? If you give a gift freely, can you ever feel resentful for not receiving one in return?

Some people are "stamp collectors," people who keep track of everything they have done and everything other people have done or not done for them. This is a difficult way to be—always keeping track, always living in a form of quid pro quo, always reminding you of the great gift they gave whenever they want you to do something.

But the truth is, if a person gives in order to get something back, no matter how much they give and how little they expect back, they are not being generous. Their action is not spiritual, it's transactional. And love is not something that can be bartered or bought and sold.

For example, Shelly was always giving things to her last boyfriend—sweet things like little gifts and cards. This was lovely. But she was always wondering when she would get something back.

"You know, I've told him so many times, in hints and

directly, that I love flowers," she complained one day. "He hasn't gotten me one flower, and we've known each other for more than a year."

"Has he done anything else?"

"He's brought me a couple of small gifts, some nice jewelry, nothing huge."

"Has he shown up for you in any other way?" I kept probing.

"When I went through that trouble dealing with cleaning up from my painkiller addiction, he was really amazing."

"So he has been generous, but just not in the one way that you think is meaningful, which is being romantic and giving the gift of flowers."

"Right. It's such a small thing, and he hasn't been able to do it. I just don't get it! He says he doesn't buy into all that romantic stuff. It's not real. He says anybody can buy flowers."

"Doesn't he have a point?"

"No! What about just doing it because it would make me feel good? Don't I deserve that?"

"But, Shelly, you're in the land of expectations. You're expecting him to conform to your idea of generosity, your idea of what a gift should look like. But when you were really down and out, almost on the brink of losing everything including your job, he showed up for you in a deep way. Isn't that generous?"

"Well, if you put that way, I guess so. But it wouldn't kill him to buy a friggin' flower once in a while." We both cracked up laughing. She saw how absurd the situation was.

It comes down to a radical acceptance of other people as they are, a radical acceptance of where they are in their development.

Generosity takes many forms. The Australian philosopher Peter Singer set up the ethical puzzle called "The Shallow Pond and the Envelope." In the first situation, a child has fallen into a shallow pond and is drowning. A person watches and considers saving the child and reflects on the inconvenience of wet, muddy clothes. In the second case, the same person receives a request by the Bengal Relief Fund to send a donation to save the lives of children overseas. To ignore the drowning child in the pond would be disgusting, most rational people would agree; to ignore an envelope from a charity would not be. But Singer's point is that the two scenes of negligence are ethically identical.

"If we can prevent something bad without sacrificing anything of comparable significance, we ought to do it," he has written. To allow harm is to do harm; it is wrong not to give money that you do not need for the most basic necessities. In an essay titled "Living High and Letting Die," the philosopher Peter Unger makes a similar point, saying that we let ourselves off the ethical hook too easily. According to Unger, we placate our consciences with an "illusion of innocence."

Not all philosophers agree with this interpretation of generosity. Colin McGinn, a philosopher at Rutgers, has called Singer's principle "positively bad, morally speaking," for "it encourages a way of life in which many important values are sacrificed to generalized altruism," and it devalues "spending one's energies on things other than helping suffering people in distant lands. . . . Just think of how much the human race would have lost if Newton and Darwin and Leonardo and Socrates had spent their time on charitable acts!"

Indeed, how can we ignore the specific and individual contributions we might be born to make in the areas of arts and sciences? How can we change our individual destiny and trade it in for a kind of moral absolutism? These are good questions, though I'm not sure they are mutually exclusive—why not do both? And what is the cost of ignoring other people in need? What is the corrosive cost to our own feeling of connection with our fellow humans when we ignore suffering? What part of ourselves do we have to shut down and numb out? And what would our planet be like if we all gave to the limit of our ability to those suffering? It would literally be transformed. It would be a different planet.

Generosity takes many forms. There is the one-on-one generosity of being generous with your partner, generous without expecting anything in return, giving a gift without ever reminding the other person that you're giving it. This can take any number of forms, from listening over and over again to the same complaints about their work to the giving of gifts. Just be certain to see the intention and the form of generosity your partner is comfortable giving and accept it, even if you think it should look like something else. In this way you will always be pleasantly surprised and appreciative; you will see the positive intent behind the gift rather than harping on the negative.

It is a matter of acceptance of the other person. Understand that accepting generosity can be as difficult as giving for some people, bringing up feelings of fear, anxiety, and vulnerability. So ask yourself, how are you at receiving? Are you gracious and open, or suspicious and demanding?

The other thing to keep in mind is that generosity is connected. So try to have a generous spirit with the world. Responding to suffering with an open heart will naturally make you a more generous person. And while absolutism, giving away everything except that which you need to survive, is admirable, blaming yourself or other people who don't is not.

Generosity is a spectrum. On the one hand is a man named Zell Kravinsky, who, after giving away his fortune of $45 million, literally donated one of his kidneys to a stranger in need. On the other hand is the typical Scrooge, rich beyond all necessity, hoarding, miserly, and not at all empathetic with other people's suffering.

Assess where you are in this spectrum, and use your relationship with your partner and the world to stretch your generosity.

Give without expecting anything in return.

Receive graciously, without feeling indebtedness.

It is one of the ways we show love.

# FEAR

## Finding the Courage to Love

*And the day came*
*when the risk*
*to remain tight in a bud*
*was more painful*
*than the risk*
*it took to blossom.*

ANAÏS NIN

Love is what we want.

Love is what we fear.

We yearn for the feeling of connectedness, the taste of nonduality, the experience of coming out of ourselves and melting with another person.

We fear the loss of that love or engulfment so much that we don't let ourselves go there. We dance around it. We avoid it. We have been burned before, and we don't want to be burned again. The definition of insanity is doing the same thing over and over and expecting different results, right?

Wrong.

As I have mentioned before, it all ends badly. Life involves suffering and death and the loss of loved ones. And fear of that is perfectly normal. Fear arises in all sorts of circumstances, as a natural and even healthy response to different situations.

But if fear is universal, what is courage?

Courage, by every definition, isn't the lack of fear. It's doing something in spite of the fear. You love in spite of the knowledge that the love will end, at the very least in death.

It is impossible to protect yourself from this kind of loss; to try to do so results in paralysis, a deadening of the heart and spirit. The axiom that you can't select the feelings you experience is true. If you are trying to prevent painful feelings, you will also prevent joyous ones. There is only one conduit to express feelings, and if it is contracted or blocked, then that's it. The amount of happiness you can feel is proportional to the amount of pain you can feel.

So how do you deal with fear? In the realm of relationship, you love anyway. Fear usually arrives on the back of a thought, like a drunk on a burro. "He doesn't like me as much as I like him," or "She's too dynamic and beautiful for me," or "He's been married before, so he's damaged goods," or "He's never been married, so he's afraid of commitment."

On and on it can go. But these are just thoughts. You don't have to go along for the ride. They come, they go, very much connected to our past experiences. Very much connected to our "story."

I was once in a relationship with a woman named

Claudia, whom I really loved. We had been through a lot of ups and downs, ins and outs. There were long periods of separation, while we each were involved in work or travel or moving to different cities or the kind of deep retreats and self-study that can only be done outside of a relationship. But mostly we were separated because Claudia would bail after three weeks of intense, sensational sex and incredible passion. We had spiritual affinity, intellectual sparks, physical chemistry, but none of that mattered. Every time we came together, she would leave. The last time we tried it again, she called. I could hear the edge in her voice.

"You know, Arthur, every time I hear your voice, my heart leaps. I mean, literally, I feel so happy, like a puppy wagging its tail."

"Okay," I said, laughing at the image, but hearing a qualifier coming. "But?"

"It's just that when we spend time together I'm really happy. When we are together it feels good." She said. "But when I'm alone, all I can do is think of reasons why we shouldn't be together. I feel driven crazy by us."

"And how does this square with what your heart feels?" I asked.

"Well, my heart feels great. But when I think about it, it seems hopeless."

"So maybe you should stop listening to this litany of thought. Recognize it as what you yourself have called 'negative mind.' "

There was a long pause.

"I battle with that every day . . . just an incredible straitjacket mind that goes off on me all the time."

"We all have thoughts all the time," I said. "I'm not saying this because I think you and I should be together. I don't know the answer to that. What I'm saying is that this negative mind, this product of severe conditioning, is affecting all aspects of your life. Right?"

"Right."

"The only thing to do is to do nothing. Watch the thought, have compassion for the fearful little girl who was so scared, who was so abused growing up. Perhaps even have a dialogue with that fearful little girl. But don't, as the adult who has so much wisdom, treat the thoughts as if they were real. That is akin to telling ghost stories to that little girl, scaring her half to death."

"But how do I get out of it? I know it is mind, but I can't seem to leave it behind."

"Differentiate between imagination about the relationship and reality. Don't get caught up in your fearful litany of 'we both are freelancers and dreamers, who's going to make sure the trains run on time?' That's simply the fearful futurizing of mind. Stay in the moment, it is your portal out of fearful thoughts."

"I can't do it, Arthur," she said again, making it the fourth time she was getting ready to leave. "I just feel too uncomfortable, too much internal conflict."

"Maybe that discomfort is an indication that love is in the house," I said. "Maybe we should take it as a barometer that there are intense feelings between us. Let's try to accept the internal conflict as a given, not something that shouldn't be there."

We spoke for quite a while about that, but nothing I could say could persuade her to keep going with the relationship. She slipped out, despite an obvious and intense connection. Claudia seemed never to be able to stay in it, honoring that connection with a commensurate amount of commitment. Her "internal conflict," as she liked to put it, was just too much.

So I tried to think of a response that was different, one that didn't blame her and get furious with her for not being able to keep her word, one that broke our usual pattern, for ultimately it's not loving to expect somebody to be where you want them to be when they are not able. That's like asking a person with a broken leg to run a marathon; it's not going to happen.

Claudia and I loved each other, but there was no way she could maintain the contact, that much was clear. I was poised to send her an "I never want to see you again" e-mail after she pulled the plug the last time. I thought it would be the most loving thing to do for myself, to just get off the merry-go-round. But how loving was it to cut her out of my life because she wasn't ready? And it never seemed to work anyway. She would call in a few months and I would greet her eagerly, completely engulfed in our connection.

But what to do? What would actually show love? Then I thought, what about acceptance? I sat with it for a few days to see if I could live with her as a friend, given all the attraction between us. I thought I could, so I called her one day to propose a friendship. When she picked up the phone, there was immediate resistance in her voice—our last conversation had ended in an argument.

"I really have to be going," she said, preempting any conversation. "It's not a good time to talk right now."

"Claudia, I know we've been fighting. We've been here before when you suddenly decide to leave. But I don't want to lose you," I said, carefully, not knowing how she would respond. "I would like to work on a friendship with you."

Silence on the phone.

"Really?" she said.

"Yes. I just don't want to lose you again. Let's work on being friends and loving each other that way. I feel we have actually been trying to be together for four years, trying to manage our own personal growth and the intensity of our connection. So let us work on friendship and trust. I don't want to possess you, I never have. My heart is open to you, my palm is open."

"This just . . . warms my heart." Claudia started to cry. "That feels so good to me. So loving."

"Really?" I said, not expecting her to melt like this. "I just want to share this experience called life with you in any form it takes."

"That feels so . . . good," Claudia said.

"We might be able to bring down the anxiety level," I said.

And so we slowly became friends. It wasn't easy, given our attraction to each other, but it was easier than saying good-bye to this person whom I loved. Gradually we got to a point of trust where she was telling me what was going on with her battle with her mind. She was secure enough in the friendship that we were able to discuss it. I was able to show up for her in ways that weren't about my needs. And she was gradually able to do the same. Who knows where it is going, but right now there is love in the house of our relationship. We are being loving with each other and out of that love may come a relationship that feels stable and secure, based on friendship.

The litmus test will be when she tells me she's seeing somebody else. But I've actually been through it with another girlfriend, Vivian, with whom I was in love. What I've noticed is that by becoming Vivian's friend and confidant and watching her torture subsequent boyfriends along the way, we've actually created a really joyous friendship.

At one point I was as wrapped up with Vivian as I am with Claudia, but now I see we were never meant to be together. After a bad breakup, I vowed never to see her again, which was tremendously painful for us both. We really loved each other, but that didn't necessarily mean we should be together. By becoming Vivian's friend, by really seeing her and accepting her as she was at the time, I was able to let our relationship become what it was supposed to be. We didn't lose each other just because I couldn't have the type of relationship I wanted when I wanted it. And in stripping down all the projection, I realized some time later that we really weren't that intellectually compatible, we really didn't want the same things or share the same values. For friends, that was fine. For lovers, it was a disaster. So my relationship with Vivian became almost a big brother/little sister friendship. And we now really enjoy each other.

Most relationships end because of fear of some sort. And most fear comes down to your relationship with your own thoughts and expectations. We often see the world as we are, not as it is. Claudia is not alone in her dynamic with her mind, not alone in believing its fears. At some point we all have it, but fear doesn't come out of nowhere. There is usually a thought before it. And from that thought comes the emotion.

We don't want to ignore the emotion when it is pure. If animal fear comes up and raises your hackles, you'd better pay attention to it. If it's in the gut and coming from pure instinct, you won't think at all, you will be propelled to act. You will cross the street or lock the doors of your car or not enter an empty alley at night. It's instinctive. Don't allow your mind any say in this kind of fear, even if it's saying you're being silly or racist or whatever. Simply act without thinking; this is the survival instinct from the gut, and its importance can't be emphasized.

Initially, within the realm of attraction and partnering, thought is usually not involved; we act on the level of instinct. And this is perfectly natural—the way it should be—chemistry usually doesn't lie. The plate tectonics of attraction moving deeply within our subconscious are the DNA of relationship. But how do you balance the head and the heart? How do you negotiate the chemical attraction, the need to bond, the mysterious pull toward certain people, with the observant mind that can make a rational decision about which person to choose? And how do you balance natural desire with neurotic thought, which is producing a fear of being hurt? In short, which do you believe, your heart, your observant mind, or your neurotic mind?

The heart must be followed, for not to follow it would mean to shut down on some important level. It would be a betrayal of ourselves to fear, and would affect us on a physical level. But along with that, the mind has its place. And if the mind's observations are ignored, if the behavior that you observe that reveals a person to be selfish or narcissistic or mean is overlooked, you proceed at your own risk.

But whether I am in a relationship that is emotionally unhealthy, or fleeing a good relationship out of fear, if I am not following my heart I will literally get sick. I usually get sick in my lungs and end up with bronchitis, or catch a stomach flu that takes forever to recover from.

Does this ever happen to you, when you talk yourself into something rather than following your true heart? Or out of something because you are afraid?

If our mind betrays our heart, our body will be in continual revolt until we are back living in harmony with our true feelings. Ironically, our very search for safety, staying in an unfulfilling relationship or avoiding any at all, will put us in an unsafe place. Our bodies are too sensitive to be shoved against the sharp edges of our mind's lie, which ultimately is telling some story that the body just doesn't buy. So a person who has made a decision against his or her feelings, out of either desire or fear, will pay a somatic price. The body will go to war with itself, in mute and silent repudiation of the mind. It will simply stop working, break down, or directly say, in ways that can be quite miserable, "Listen to me."

So how does one differentiate between useful thought, which is making useful observations, and neurotic thought, which is a product of fear?

If there is a contest between heart and mind, simply sit still and pull your awareness fully into the present moment. Don't allow your mind to pull you into "what ifs" about the future or "if only" about the past. Trust your direct experience with the other person moment by moment. This means trusting both the observations that your mind makes about their behavior in the moment and trusting the feelings you have about them, *when you are with them*. View the thoughts that arise in their absence as suspect.

But understand that most of the time we want to explore what there is to explore with a new lover. We want to let it run its course. And most of us will have to overcome some barrier due to fear. And most of this fear is generated from the mind.

So, like a rocket leaving the earth's atmosphere, it will

take some attention and energy to get beyond this fear. Go for the full ride.

If you get quiet enough, you will *know*.

If you wake yourself up into each moment, you will *know*.

Have the courage to trust that knowing.

Have the courage to trust love when it shows up on your doorstep.

# BLAME

## Ignoring Your Spiritual Journey

Reconciliation is to understand both sides; to go to one
side and describe the suffering being endured by the
other side, and then go to the other side and describe
the suffering being endured by the first side.

THICH NHAT HANH

There are some people in the New Age world who believe
in something they call "agreement reality." It's the idea that
the entire world exists because everybody in it agrees to
agree that it does. Everything you see or hear or experience is an illusion; we are all creating our reality. If we
stopped believing it, it would evaporate like a dream.

My direct experience of this is that it's nonsense. Even
though everything we look at is, in fact, mostly space—
fast-moving electrons, protons, quarks—which gives the
illusion of solidity, a car hitting you as you cross the street
will feel mighty solid. These teachings are not about adding

belief systems, but are about releasing them, allowing you to see reality as it is, not as you think it should be. Not a reality based on concepts, but one based on your direct experience.

In my first book, *City Dharma,* I talked about this concept of "creating your reality" as it originated in the New Age community. In the case of cancer patients, for instance, the idea that somehow they "manifested" their cancer by what they thought and by their attitude toward life is prevalent in many forms of New Age spirituality. According to that way of thinking, if this is true, then the opposite must also be true. If you think positive thoughts about manifesting wealth or a job or anything you desire, then it will happen. A whole industry has arisen around selling this idea: books, videos, and seminars on how to "manifest" power, success, etc.

I would say that this concept is true up to a point. One's attitude obviously has a lot to do with how people react to you and with how much you enjoy life. But the idea that you are "creating" cancer by your thoughts denies such realities as genetic predisposition. You can eat all the salad you want, but if that genetic time bomb is set to go off, thinking positive thoughts is not going to stop it.

This comes down the illusion of control. Many forms of spirituality profess to give you control in some way over the vagaries of life and death. If you act a certain way, you will be able to control reality, either now or in the afterlife. Be good and go to heaven, be bad and go to hell. However, as I've mentioned before, control is an illusion. What is important is to learn how to live with the ambiguity of existence. Accept uncertainty and change for what they are, intrinsic aspects of life.

The one arena where we *do* create our own reality is in interpersonal relationships. We choose the people with whom we get involved, either consciously or unconsciously. They are a mirror of our own interior landscape.

So, when we blame our partners for their failings, are we not blaming some part of ourselves? In fact, isn't it true that the thing that bothers us the most about other people is usually something within ourselves? If you are irritated or upset by somebody's behavior, if you find yourself being extremely reactive to your partner or another person, it is worthwhile to look within and find that part of yourself. The things we hate about other people are the things we hate about ourselves, and usually when we blame somebody else for something, we are not taking the time to look within.

When I am triggered by somebody, I ask the question of myself, what is it within me that is so reactive? Why? It is not them, they are just who they are. It is me, my feelings and reactivity. This is a freer way to look at it rather than thinking you are at the mercy of other people. You are not.

The thing about blaming our partners is that underneath it is the idea that if they would just change, we could finally be happy. You might as well put yourself in psychic jail and give the key to somebody else.

And the other half of this dynamic is the fantasy that somewhere out there is the perfect partner. But they are impossible to compete with because they are a *fantasy*. It is the very nature of fantasies to be perfect. But in reality there is no such person; scratch the surface of anybody and you will discover that. So figure it out with your partner, especially if they are willing. And even if they are not, use the relationship to grow spiritually, for even the worst relationships offer that—an opportunity to expand and deepen the qualities of compassion and honesty.

Fantasy is also a form of blaming your partner for not being perfect.

Annie and Ken had this kind of dynamic. They were crazy about each other and had a lot in common. Both were artistic; they loved to read and talk about big ideas. They were intellectually compatible and made each other laugh a lot. They lived together and Ken wanted to get married, but there was just one problem: Annie was completely worried about money. She didn't think they made enough and secretly blamed Ken, who was a schoolteacher, for not being more successful. Even though they lived a comfortable existence, she was worried all the time about how they would survive. It was preventing her from saying yes to a potentially fulfilling marriage.

But Ken had a very steady job. He had always worked and made money. Annie, who was a writer, was the one who worked periodically. Her income was unreliable, yet she blamed Ken for their occasional financial problems. If she felt more capable of taking care of herself financially, she would probably not be so hard on Ken.

And with Annie, if you peeled back another layer, there was the fantasy that somewhere out there was somebody with the same chemistry, intellectual affinity, and love, but with a couple million dollars. How was Ken going to live up to this fantasy when all he could offer was a working relationship? He wasn't a perfect human being, he couldn't compete with unreality. They are still working it out as Annie slowly begins to realize that underneath her blaming Ken and her fantasy ideology is a deep fear of intimacy.

Blame is ultimately a way to avoid looking at yourself.

Every relationship has two people in it who create the dynamic—every single one, even the ones that seem lop-sidedly horrific. At the very least, there is collusion be-tween the two people playing complementary roles in order to create a system. Often the people in the system don't even know it's been created. They don't see the dy-namic at play. This is why therapists can be useful; they are outside of the system. It is the same reason why companies hire management consultants to tell them what they them-selves cannot see.

If you are blaming your partner, you are missing oppor-tunities to grow. For everything you don't like about them, you don't like about yourself. The answer to this impulse toward blame is deep acceptance, of yourself and your partner. Let them be who they are—accept their faults, ac-cept your own.

Both you and they are perfect embodiments of con-sciousness. They are perfectly and busily being exactly who they are meant to be. Who are you to change them? Who are you to blame them for being who they are?

Pointing the finger never changes anything, and it cre-ates a sense of separation that prevents mutual understand-ing and acceptance.

Let it go.

# FLEEING
# FROM LOVE

## Staying When the Going Gets Good

*To fear love is to fear life, and those who fear life
are already three parts dead.*

BERTRAND RUSSELL

"I don't know, every time things seem to be going well, I do something to sabotage it," my friend Jackie told me as she and I huffed up the trail in the Santa Monica Mountains. "Like . . . I want to pull the trigger and end it before he does."

"Why?" I really wanted to hear what she said, because I've gone out with people like her. Too many people like her. "I mean, if it's good, why not just enjoy it?"

"I don't know. I just guess I think it can't last, so I'd rather end it myself."

In a nutshell, this is the unseen effect of growing up in a

dysfunctional, alcoholic family, which was Jackie's experience, along with that of millions of other people. If you grew up in an environment where any happiness was short-lived, where the other shoe was going to drop any minute due to an alcoholic or rage-aholic bender, where there was no guarantee that you would get through the day without being hit, then you tend to learn that the happiness you have is fleeting. So in trying to give yourself a semblance of control, you end the happiness yourself. At least then it *wasn't something done to you*. You are not a victim.

But you are a victim of your conditioning.

And the truth is that happiness is fleeting, anyway. Like all things in life. We all know we are going to die, but why end it early?

"You know," I said to Jackie, "I fell in madly in love with a girl who told me a story once. When she was a girl she used to lie in bed with a full glass of water on the nightstand. She would wake up in the middle of the night and she'd be so thirsty. The water was right there, in arm's reach. But she wouldn't drink it. She would sit in the dark and go thirsty."

"But why?"

"I could ask you the same thing," I said, pausing to view the ocean, which glittered out before us. "I guess on some level she wanted to prove to herself that she could go without."

"But it's like cutting off your nose to spite your face."

"Yes. I pointed that out to her. And then I said that I was that tall glass of water and why couldn't she reach out and take what she desired."

"You're too short to be a tall glass of water."

We looked at each other and laughed.

"Allow me my small delusions," I said. "The point I'm trying to make is that self-denial and asceticism is not necessarily part of a spiritual path. It usually comes down to fear of the sloppy, messy, less than perfect aspects of relationship."

"Yes, I know," Jackie sighed, squatting to adjust her shoelace. "But it's just something I do all the time. I don't know what to do, how to get out of it."

"You're stuck telling yourself that every time you experience happiness it's going to end horribly."

"Yes. Then I feel a lot of anxiety. I feel like I have to do something."

"But why? Why not, as the Tao says, do nothing? Simply watch the thoughts that come up. Why believe that they will be true?" I looked at her.

"But you yourself have said that happiness is fleeting. Why shouldn't I take control of when it's going to end?"

"Pleasure comes and goes. Happiness is deeper, but even that comes and goes. *Everything* comes and goes. That doesn't mean you kick the very person that is causing you happiness out of your life." We stopped to admire the view.

"Look at this view, this hike, this time we are spending together. It produces happiness. We are looking at a beautiful view, talking about meaningful things, enjoying nature. Everything is perfect. Later we might be stuck in traffic," I said. "And there's no reason that won't be perfect, too."

"How?"

"By accepting that everything, and I mean *everything,* is ephemeral. Everything passes: people, jobs, work, planets . . . Nothing lasts. Accept that basic truth and become free to enjoy what is here right now. Don't allow the mind to rob you of it. "

Jackie looked at me and nodded. She gave me a big hug.

"I appreciate you right now."

"Thanks. And I you," I said. "Any desire to pick a fight and end this moment?"

"None."

"Good. Let's walk down the mountain in silence. Just observe the thoughts that come up and bring your attention to each step down this beautiful mountain."

"Fantastic idea."

And so we did.

Once you accept that nothing lasts forever, you become free of trying to hold on to it. You also liberate yourself from self-denial.

You simply accept the joy each moment brings, no matter what is happening. For each moment of life, of mere existence, is a privilege.

For there are only a finite number of them in a life.

# LISTEN UP!

## Present Moment Listening

The deepest Hunger of the
human soul is to be understood.
The deepest hunger of the human body is for air.
If you can listen to another person, in depth, until they
feel understood, it's the equivalent of giving them air.

STEVEN COVEY

Most couples who have been together for a long time point
to communication as an important ingredient in their relationships, if not the most important. But what exactly does
good communication mean? Does it mean you can say anything to your partner? Or does it mean that you never want
to say the thing that can't be unsaid?

One of the ways in which you can take the stars from
your eyes and really see another person is to simply listen
to them, to give them the gift of your full undivided attention without judgment or agenda. Don't be thinking about

how you might be able to help them, or what you're going to say when they stop talking. Be receptive, but not passive. Actively listen, without being aware of being a "listener."

What does this mean? It means that you are not looking at your partner and thinking that what he's saying is right or wrong, true or untrue, good or bad. It simply *is*. Listen as though you're just trying to understand what the other person is saying. Literally be like a reporter trying to get the facts of what the other person is trying to communicate, without prejudgment or opinion. This frees you up to become totally present for your partner.

I can hear some of you saying that that's impossible! How can you listen without forming an opinion, argument, or rebuttal? To which I would say that it's impossible to truly listen while thinking. So listening without any reference back to "me" or "my thoughts"—listening without any sense of "I" is the only way in which you can truly listen as opposed to simply hearing. This is, not surprisingly, a simple and very effective way to bring you into the present moment and make you drop your story.

Many problems in a relationship result from a back-and-forth, he-said-she-said power struggle. The focus is on trying to convince or change your partner, or trying to make the other person wrong and make you right. But think about it for a moment. If you have successfully made somebody "wrong," how are they going to feel? When you make somebody wrong, they will hold resentment and will wait, perhaps unconsciously, to make you wrong. And so goes the endless power struggle that eliminates any chance of peace in the relationship. As soon as you insert the "I think" into the process of listening, you are out of the moment.

Men often make the mistake of trying to solve the problems of their partner. It's a natural impulse for us. We are "doers." But often what women want is simply to give voice to what is bothering them, to be heard. Sometimes this happens even within a spiritual context. One day as I was coming out of teaching a yoga class, I met Clara, one of my students, walking out of the parking lot.

"How are you?" I asked as we fell into step with each other.

"Oh . . . you know. Just having one of those days. Know what I mean? Just not feeling right."

"Yes, that can happen," I said. We approached the top of the staircase. I glanced at her face and saw a state that I recognized. Clara's pretty face was plagued by thoughts. Suffering from the nonstop nattering of her mind, she couldn't wake up into the moment. As we stood at the top of the stairs, I recognized the suffering state, having been there myself, and I thought I could help.

"Do you want to change your mood by the time we reach the bottom of the stairs?" I asked the question lightly, not wanting to push her. I had in mind a simple mindfulness exercise, one in which each step you take becomes a call to wakefulness in the present moment. With each step down, you focus your awareness in the NOW, using the staircase as a metaphor for descending out of the "small self" of nonstop thought and into the larger self of universal consciousness. It's a simple exercise, always available to you, no matter what you are doing. By focusing your attention on the task at hand, by allowing yourself to be absorbed in the moment with what is happening, no matter what it is, the mind's madness gets crowded out by the vibrancy of NOW.

Clara was having none of it.

"No . . . that's okay. I'm fine."

"Oh. Okay," I said, surprised.

"See you later." She stepped quickly down the stairs and disappeared out the door.

Instead of simply listening, I'd gone into "teacher" mode. I tried to fix her problem. This is fine if you are in a situation where you are in a student/teacher relationship and given permission to teach. If we had been in one of my weekly dharma conversations, my response would have been perfectly legitimate. But we weren't. All Clara needed was a sympathetic ear, a "Yes, I hear you, some days are like that." That would have been the most empathic response.

Now comes the tricky part of this. Even if you know you're right, even if you can see that another person's suffering is being *caused* by them, even if you know how you can truly help them, most of the time the wiser path is simply to listen. If they want advice, they will ask for it.

This is just one way in which it is better just to listen to somebody who is trying to communicate with you.

Become listening, but not a *listener*. Become invisible to yourself.

In this way, you can really show up for your partner in the present moment.

# PART FOUR

# The Middle

## The End of the Beginning or the Beginning of the End?

# PERFECTIONISM AND POWER STRUGGLES

## Don't Play That Game

Tell me what a man finds sexually attractive and
I will tell you his entire philosophy of life.
Show me the woman he sleeps with and I will
tell you his valuation of himself.

AYN RAND

I once had a girlfriend who never wanted to fight. She was
a sweet person who hated conflict and didn't want to do
anything that would tarnish the relationship. She, in what
seemed like a beautiful way, never wanted to say the thing
that couldn't be unsaid, never wanted to do an insensitive
deed that couldn't be undone. She wanted to keep our relationship whole and spiritual.

But some conflict is a natural part of any relationship, and conflict avoidance isn't necessarily "spiritual." Unresolved psychological issues that leak out in the form of passive aggressiveness are common in this situation. And while I agree that it is better not to go to a place, in either word or deed, that is impossible to return from, people are all too human and imperfect. And expecting there to be no conflict is not real; it isn't that conflict doesn't happen, it's how that conflict is negotiated that counts.

Expecting perfectionism in oneself or another is a disease, usually as a result of growing up in a dysfunctional family (suffering from the effects of addiction or mental illness or abuse). The young child is conditioned to tiptoe around the explosive parents, trying to get it just right, because if they get everything just right, then the parents won't get drunk or abuse them or abuse each other. So they are perfect, very chipper, and high achievers. They don't learn to live with difficult emotions. Conflict means the end of the world, so it is to be avoided at all cost.

There is a so-called "spiritual" side of this. Because we're all supposed to be like the Buddha, that is, peaceful all the time while smiling beatifically, conflict is seen as bad. We are supposed to be perfect; that's the whole point of a spiritual path, right? But haven't we all met the spiritual dude who's got a patina of peace and harmony going? He wears a persona masking unresolved issues that bubble to the surface when he sleeps with his yoga student or embezzles from his charity.

Living with this kind of perfectionism is exhausting for the person and exhausting for the people around him. You can never get to know the real person behind the persona. And as far as holding up the persona is concerned, presenting it to the world like a fine set of clothes, what's the point? People will only interact with what you offer them, ultimately leaving you alone and lonely. So dare to be who you really are, warts and all. Let it out and make yourself human. It is in our common humanity that we find common ground.

I know that with my girlfriend the perfectionism became so tight and relentless that it was like wearing a strait-jacket. We never fought until we broke up. There was no way for the normal tension in a relationship to relieve itself.

The point is to find a person who will disappoint you in ways that are tolerable, because everyone will disappoint you somehow. Accept that as a truism: people are imperfect. We all make mistakes. But it is in choosing wisely the person you give your heart to that you can find somebody who will disappoint you in ways you can live with. You can't deal with adultery, but you can live with occasional bouts of self-absorption. Know your own baseline and stick to it.

Conversely, revealing enough of yourself and accepting that at some time you are going to hurt or disappoint your partner is a part of mature love. If neither side expects perfection, then a working relationship is possible. Conflict is negotiated and resolved. Otherwise you are in a power struggle to get the other person to be perfect in your eyes. This is where most couples get stuck. Sometimes a relationship can be a thirty-year power struggle, with each party trying to get the other to be something they are not.

Yeah, yeah, you might be saying, easier said than done; but what about the insane nature of love? What about the fact that the very thing that has wounded you before is what attracts you now? How do you get around the plate tectonics of interlocking dysfunction? What about the fact that you fall in love with exactly the wrong person, to whom you are inexplicably drawn? Well, there's no easy, pat answer to that. But each go-round gives you another chance to work it out, both spiritually and psychologically. You are drawn to that person to heal the original wound.

We all have our poison, so to speak. I mean, I always fall for highly intelligent, beautiful, extremely sensitive women with a predilection toward addiction. But as I evolve, I have chosen (or skipped entirely) this form of the poison that attracts me. The pull may still be strong, but it is less so. Which is not to say it ever fully goes away—it just gets more subtle. The intensity of the lessons I am learning in each relationship gets less severe. There is an evolution.

Ideally, we are in relationship as a form of celebration. But we are also in it as a way to grow spiritually. This growth may often be painful, but it is also inherently useful. Your partner's extreme sensitivity may stimulate your gentleness. Their dependence may trigger your patience. Their struggles may help you develop your compassion.

This is the dance of love and intimacy. This is the way we evolve spiritually. The trick is to know what is evolving you spiritually and what is devolving you in a mismatch in which you are rubbing each other raw. The answer to that is time. If you are grinding it out, unhappy, trying to change each other and bringing out the worst in each other, then perhaps the spiritual lesson is to move on.

Let's face it, being in a relationship, living with somebody all the time, seeing them all the time whether you feel like seeing them or not, can be difficult under the best of circumstances. There is a lot of compromise involved. But if you are trying to change some intrinsic part of their personality, trying to turn an introvert into an extrovert, a lone wolf into a family man, or a philosopher into a business tycoon, then you are in for a long slog. You are constantly in a form of judgment, which creates separation, both with your partner and with the rest of the world. This requires a shift in the paradigm through which we view the world:

From "me" to "we."

From "mine" to "ours."

From "one" to "all."

Acceptance of what is, rather than what you want things to be, is a cornerstone of the dharma. Acceptance of other people, allowing them to be who they are, without judgment, is a cornerstone of happy interpersonal relationship. This is what it means to be loving. There is no room for perfectionism, either in other people or ourselves.

There just is what is.

# ADULTERY

## The End or a New Beginning?

*A successful marriage is an edifice
that must be rebuilt every day.*

ANDRÉ MAUROIS

Adultery is common and it's not gender-specific—60 percent of the men in America commit adultery, but so do 40 percent of the women. These are huge numbers, and you could write an entire book about adultery in all its forms. There is the compulsive adultery of the sex addict. There is the adultery of the man who is in a sexless relationship. There is adultery that might arise from "boredom," as partners take each other for granted. Or the adultery of the woman who married an older man for security and finds herself attracted to the pool guy. Or the insane chemical connection that can happen between two people, resulting in an explosion of desire that obliterates everything in its path.

But certain similarities run through all adultery. One is not telling the whole truth. The other is self-justification. Usually, adultery means that somebody is not telling the truth, either to himself or to his partner. There is some breakdown in communication. For committing adultery is a passive way of saying "I'm not happy" with this relationship, and an even deeper way of communicating that a person is not happy with herself. She is presenting a happy front, all the while smuggling her emotions out of the relationship.

They have not "told the truth faster." And there is usually a reason for it.

Like the extreme case of Carrie, who is committing adultery as a mission of mercy. Her old friend John is suffering from ALS (Lou Gehrig's disease) and is losing control of his muscle movement. He is essentially paralyzed from the neck down, and is on a respirator. Every day, when the batteries on his respirator die, there is a scramble to get them changed so he can breathe again. Someday, perhaps soon, his respiration will stop and he will suffocate.

Surprisingly, in the middle of this physical breakdown, John can still have an orgasm. But Lydia, his wife of one year, won't have anything to do with him sexually. She just won't talk about it. It's an incredibly difficult time for her and John, who got married after he was diagnosed. They knew he was going to have anywhere from two to five years to live, and it is a testament to their love that they went ahead and got married anyway. Sometimes ALS victims can live longer, with the symptoms abating or slowing. In a tiny percentage they even reverse. But John isn't in this lucky group. His health deteriorated quickly and soon he was unable to move and required a full-time nurse.

Carrie would occasionally come over and keep him company, giving Lydia some time off to go out with friends.

This was when John asked Carrie to give him a hand job.

Now, these two were old friends and at one time had toyed with the idea of being lovers, but didn't go there. Still, they were very close, and at first Carrie was shocked.

"John!"

"She doesn't touch me anymore," John complained. "She doesn't see me as a sexual being anymore. I've got nothing to look forward to."

After a long discussion, Carrie complied. And she did it again on her next visit as well. When she told me about it, I pointed out that she was committing adultery.

"Well, I don't see it that way," Carrie said, immediately getting defensive. "You can say what you want, and society can have its judgments, but the bottom line is it's a mission of mercy."

"Really?" I said. "Tell me about that."

"It's completely mechanical. I don't get turned on at all. It's just to give him a moment of pleasure. You know, give a dying man a moment of pleasure."

We looked at each other and couldn't avoid laughing at how absurd and melodramatic it sounded.

"How very *World According to Garp* of you," I said, referring the John Irving novel in which a nurse gets herself impregnated by a paralyzed, out-of-his-mind veteran, who is tumescent each night on her shift.

"Yeah, well, don't give me a hard time about it. The poor guy doesn't have sex anymore."

"You know, I'm not judging you. I'm just saying that given your history of being with married men, I think it's worth looking at." Carrie had been the "other woman" a few times before. "How do you know you're not just rationalizing what you're doing? I mean, it sounds like it's altruistic, that there's no harm, no foul here, but is that true?"

Carrie stared at me, annoyed.

"I don't care what you say, it's not harming anybody."

"But how do you know? Maybe it's preventing John from having a truthful conversation with his wife about his needs. And what if she found out? How would she feel? How would you feel? I'm concerned for you and this pattern of yours of not getting what you deserve."

"I don't know," Carrie murmured, suddenly upset, tears welling in her eyes. "I just wasn't thinking about it like that. I was just trying to help him. He's in such . . . he's feeling so bad all the time. I just wanted to make him feel good . . ."

Carrie's voice trailed off as she broke into tears.

"What's wrong with that?" Carrie wiped her eyes. "I mean, for fuck's sake, he's thirty years old. He just got married and had his whole life ahead of him. Now . . ."

She stopped, too choked up to speak.

"Now?" I asked.

"Now what's he got to look forward to? Somebody wiping his ass because he can't do it himself?"

We stared at each other for a long moment in silence.

"I understand," I said, choosing my words carefully. "Sex—the sexual drive—is emblematic of life. He wants to feel alive, you want him to live . . . I'm not judging you. I understand where it's coming from."

"We're not hurting anybody. His wife will never know. He's dying!" With that Carrie broke down, and began to sob again.

We talked about it for a long time after that, and I didn't have any easy answers. I knew that her actions were tied up in deeper emotional needs and tendencies on her part, coupled with the intense feelings brought up by her friend's disease—she wanted to give him *life*. Could this be a case where the rules didn't apply?

It goes back to that old freshman question of a tree falling in the woods—if nobody is there to hear it, does it make a sound? If adultery is committed and the spouse never finds out, is any harm being done?

The answer is yes, of course, even in this unusual case. Keeping a secret affects the reality of the relationship. It warps the playing field and discards the bond and contract between monogamous couples. And the other person always knows. Deep down they know, because that secret is an invisible barrier to intimacy.

In Carrie's case, if she didn't have a history of being the other woman, perhaps, in some alternate world, a case could be made that what she was doing was a mission of mercy. But she did have this history. She did have this feeling that deep down she was only valuable for what she could give sexually.

It wasn't clean.

"How do you feel afterward?" I asked her, after she had regained her composure.

"I feel . . . sad," she said.

"I think maybe that's your answer," I said. "You've got to let him live the life he chose for himself, with the woman he chose it with. The fact that he's ill doesn't change it. She married him knowing that he had a terminal disease. That takes an act of love and courage that is almost hard to fathom. Honor that, even if, in his own sickness and despair, he doesn't want to."

Carrie nodded.

"I guess . . ." she murmured.

She never was sexual again with John. His health continues to deteriorate, and I don't know if he ever told his wife about Carrie, or if his wife ever again engaged him sexually; but either way, Carrie was back in her own integrity and acting in her own best interests.

I can remember one serious relationship I had with a woman who told me, when we were in the throes of breaking up, that she'd slept with her best friend, a married woman. The reason we were breaking up was that I felt we had reached a plateau in our intimacy. I felt that she was withholding deeper levels of herself. She claimed that she was waiting for us to get married in order to allow herself to go deeper into intimacy. I argued that I felt more comfortable if the intimacy came first and then the commitment to marriage. I thought marriage was an outgrowth of the intimacy, she thought the opposite.

In retrospect, we were both probably equally right and wrong. A commitment like marriage creates more intimacy, but it's difficult to make such a commitment unless both are feeling the intimacy first.

Into this situation enters a woman with whom I thought I had fallen in love. I definitely fell into a state of infatuation with her. Although we never slept together until two years after my relationship had ended, she was a catalyst for the breakup. I thought we had fallen in love, but the truth for her was that I was simply a dalliance. While I was busy ending my troubled relationship to be with her, she was busy starting another one with somebody else.

Meanwhile, my girlfriend was denying that she had ever cheated on me with her best friend. I wasn't actually that upset by her actions. If she had one night in a hot tub with her close friend, this was not particularly threatening. She obviously got something from the encounter that I, as a man, couldn't give her. But she kept using that exact reasoning to insist that it didn't count as cheating because it was with somebody of the same sex. Meanwhile, I had cheated on her emotionally with another woman, even though there was no sex between us.

Again, we were both a little right and a little wrong. Which comes down to another point about fidelity: it's often a subjective, eye-of-the-beholder thing. But the bottom line is that in either case it was a matter of withholding important information from the person we loved. And we are connected to our partners in ways unimaginable, so that the truth will out. It may take years, but eventually the truth will be heard.

Given that adultery is commonplace, does it need to be the end of the relationship? Obviously not. Sometimes it is a way to move through the problems that adultery symbolizes: a lack of communication or some unexpressed anger. If the issues are addressed, a relationship most certainly can survive. It can be an opportunity to practice forgiveness and compassion. Still, the wounds that come from adultery are so deep that they always leave a scar, one that can take years to heal.

Which brings me to the issue of guilt. When is it time to let go of guilt after doing something that deviates from your integrity? When do you let yourself off the hook? I think guilt is not a useful response. Remorse and chagrin are natural, but guilt doesn't effect any change in a meaningful way. Releasing guilt can't really happen until you come clean with the injured party, sincerely making amends. But if you have cheated on your spouse, telling them and apologizing from the bottom of your heart is only part of it. *Then you must do the work it takes to change the behavior.* Figuring out why you did it and facing the deepest part of yourself is the real work. This doesn't mean your partner will forgive you. It may take a long time and you will just have to wait it out. But after you have sincerely made amends and worked through the (often unconscious) reasons for your behavior, it is time to come to compassion for yourself and your conditioning.

In realizing the dharma, there is a deeper understanding of the connectivity of all things. It's as if the universe pulls back her veil and reveals the levers and strings and gears that make the whole thing work. Much of this is revealed through what we call intuition, the sense we have that something isn't right. Most of us ignore this intuition because we are so invested in a reality that we want to see. We want to be in love or we want to believe our spouse is faithful.

It is important to continue to strip ourselves of our own illusions, whether about ourselves and our motivations or about our partner.

To be awake is to understand that every action you take or don't take, especially in the arena of fidelity and relationship, matters. For even if nobody else knows, *you know.* And it affects how you feel about yourself and your sense of connection with the world.

# THE GRASS IS ALWAYS GREENER

## Dealing with Attraction to Others

*A man can sleep around, no questions asked, but if a woman makes nineteen or twenty mistakes she's a tramp.*

JOAN RIVERS

So, how do you deal with attraction to other people when you are in a monogamous relationship? What do we do about all those beautiful people we encounter in the course of daily life? People who don't leave their laundry on the floor and chew with their mouth open when they've had too much to drink or leave the cap off the toothpaste? In short, people who are not our partner.

In America we are fed a constant diet of commercials touting everything from tires to treadmills and using, in ways both subtle and overt, sex to sell them. The implied message in a beer commercial is that if you buy this beer, hot babes will be all over you. Eat these potato chips and you will be ravaged by a sex-starved supermodel! In a society that is inherently conservative and even puritanical, ironically sex is used as a come-on to sell everything.

It is an overheated environment that pours thousands of hours of advertising into our heads and hopelessly conditions us without our awareness. Many men and women are walking around in their heads labeling the opposite sex as "hot" or "not"—there's even a website where you can post a picture and find out if people think you're "hot" or "not."

In this environment of nonstop titillation, how do we stay awake when we encounter somebody whom we do consider "hot"? Perhaps it's somebody at work that's coming on to you while your partner is out of town on a business trip. Perhaps in the hothouse environment of a creative partnership, other sparks start to fly.

You are attracted, but it's inappropriate.

What do you do?

Defuse it. That's all it takes. Acknowledge it, and it disappears like fog in the hot sun.

So many times the attraction is really about something else. If you get quiet with it, and let yourself feel what is going on in the moment underneath the attraction, you will realize that it might not be about sex at all. It was about taking advantage of a person who needs something else, perhaps friendship, perhaps care, or maybe simply somebody to listen to them. For sex is often used addictively to avoid difficult feelings or to feel good from the outside or simply to get love.

This was a lesson I learned early in my life.

I once worked as manager of a restaurant. It was in Newport, Rhode Island, during the America's Cup summer of 1983, and I was working in the most popular restaurant in town. Right on the water, The Clark Cook House had a three-star formal dining room, a disco in the basement, a café on the lower deck, and a champagne bar called SkyBar on the upper deck. The party was in high gear, with the likes of Andy Warhol and Malcolm Forbes dropping in. I was twenty-three, still in college after traveling for a couple of years, and had about thirty other college kids working for me. I was the gatekeeper, controlling access to the exclusive deck.

We were being tipped with cocaine, AIDS was in the future, and everybody was sleeping with everybody. In a town loaded with Australians, Italians, and French, it was the international party to end all parties.

Enter Sabrina. From a local prominent family, she was very beautiful and vivacious, and came to work as a hostess in the café. She looked nineteen but was actually sixteen and prone to impulsive behavior. After a couple of weeks, Sabrina developed a crush on me. It was a typical infatuation of the kind a younger girl might get on an older guy in college, except she was relentless in her pursuit.

And she was beautiful.

At the time I was a marathoner and would take long runs around the ten-mile Mansion loop. Sabrina saw me one day while riding her bike, and she began to keep pace for me while I ran, making it a daily routine. She talked endlessly about nothing—I mostly listened, as I was running. Sabrina was always inviting me to go to this party or that event, but underneath her vivaciousness, and her sexualized approach to men, I sensed a really lonely and sad girl.

"Why won't you ever come to any of the beach keggers I

ask you to?" she said one day, her feet up on the handlebars, coasting as I ran. "We could drink beer and skinny-dip."

"Listen," I said, huffing a bit. "I've wanted to talk to you about this. We're never going to get involved. It's not going to happen."

"Don't you find me attractive?" she asked. I looked at her long blond hair flowing in the breeze, her taut and tan body.

"Of course I find you attractive! I'm not dead," I said. "But it's not appropriate. I'm too old for you."

"But they're all such children."

"Like you," I said. "You're still a child."

"I am not!" Sabrina was indignant. "You're only six years older than me."

"Seven. I'm seven years older. It's not going to happen."

"I think you really want to, but you're afraid."

"Yeah, afraid of jail, for one thing," I said. "Let's work on a friendship here. Deal? You can be my running coach, keep me from slacking off."

"Sounds thrilling."

She was precocious, and we talked about it some more as she argued her case. It would have been so easy to take advantage of her; she looked older than her years and was in many ways ripe for the picking. Our attraction for each other never went away, but once we acknowledged it, we were able to develop a little sister/big brother relationship. I heard all about the troubles she had with her parents, who weren't around. After a while she revealed a secret she hadn't told anybody, about her uncle who had sexually abused her when she was ten. She sobbed in my arms when she told me. She was a young woman who needed to be heard, but didn't know how to go about it except through her sexuality, for this was the way she had gotten attention and approval.

This has repeated itself over the years in many forms, in which I was the "crusher" or the "crushee." I'm sure if you think about it, there have been many times where the attraction was there and you acted on it and then wished you hadn't, because at the heart of the other person's actions was really a cry for love or attention or help.

The point is that desire exists. We are not oblivious. We have eyes. Nor can we avoid or sublimate it, because like a mushroom it grows in the dark. The absolute best thing is to throw light on it. If it is an attraction that would be inappropriate to act on, try acknowledging it to the other person. Perhaps acknowledge it to your partner, depending upon whether you have that level of honesty. It is in acknowledging the attraction and talking about it honestly that you take the allure out of the forbidden fruit.

Bring it out in the open and it dissipates.

Hide it or play games and it grows.

# CHANGE

## Allow It, Don't Force It

This isn't good or bad. It's just the way of things.
Nothing stays the same.

REAL LIVE PREACHER

Absolutely everything in the world is constantly changing from moment to moment.

This is true on a material level and on a spiritual level. Trees grow and decay, buildings deteriorate, people die, most of the cells in our body are replaced every four months, stars collapse, and every moment gives us a completely different reality unlike any other that has existed before on the planet. And the only way to experience this reality fully is to come fully into the present moment. Otherwise "reality" is changed and gone, set in the stone of the past. The NOW is the only fluid moment, and in it, change is constant.

So why do we have such a hard time dealing with change in a relationship? Why do we expect our lovers to stay the same and our relationships to stay the same? If change is a constant, why not allow it, letting relationships grow and change and evolve, perhaps even evolve out of a romantic form?

And on the other side of the coin, if you want your partner to change, why would you want to force it?

People will change at their own rate and only if they really, really want it. This is not to say that a relationship doesn't bring about change on both sides. We are there, after all, to polish each other smooth.

But if you try to change somebody before they are ready, you are not being loving. And if you try to keep somebody from growing because you don't want to see them change, then you are not being loving.

So, what is the most loving way to be with your partner?

Allow it. Allow them to be who they are. Allow them to change. That is what love is: radical acceptance of your lover. Support them in their efforts to grow, but don't try to make them grow. It's as simple as that.

My friend Alan met a woman a year ago who was just getting sober in Alcoholics Anonymous. Suzie had been a binge drinker for years. As a highly successful software salesperson, she was a functioning alcoholic. When she finally realized that she had a problem, she started going to AA meetings. A month later she met Alan, and sparks started to fly for both of them and they fell madly in love.

"I'm not supposed to be in a new relationship for a year," Suzie said to Alan. "It's one of the tenets of the program."

"But what about the connection we have?" Alan protested. "It's so huge, why can't we honor that?"

"I'm not ready," Suzie said. "I need to be alone for a year and figure out what's going on with me and the drinking."

But Alan was persistent and Suzie relented. She too really wanted to follow their connection. For a few weeks all seemed to be going well, until Alan showed up at my door looking completely bereft.

"She ended it," Alan said, morose. "She just sent me an e-mail and ended it. I can't believe it."

"She didn't give a reason?" I asked.

"She said she wasn't ready." Alan rolled his eyes. "I think she's just scared of the connection we have. She's hiding behind AA."

"It is a tenet of the program—no relationships in the first year," I said. "But does it even matter which it is?"

"Huh?"

"Does it matter if she's scared or if she's sincerely pursuing her program in AA or if she's hiding behind it?" I asked. "She's simply unavailable—that's all you need to know."

"I thought the rules didn't apply to us." Alan was passionate. "We never felt for another human being the way we feel together. I guess the rules do apply."

"She's just trying to change and isn't ready to be with you," I said. "I went through a similar thing with a girlfriend. Why don't you try to support that change, rather than looking at it from your needs? That made a difference for me. It's a matter of accepting where your partner is at."

"But I miss her!" Alan said.

"I know," I said quietly. "I know. But if you're meant to be together, you'll be together. If not, there's nothing you can do to make her ready."

Alan nodded, still unconvinced. "Yeah . . . I guess."

"The thing to remember is that nobody looks at himself as a villain, ruining other people's lives or betraying their love," I said. "Suzie's higher self wants to commit, wants to surrender, but you have to understand that she is doing the best she can with what she has right now. You've got to see her as she is, not how you think she should be."

"I know . . . I know. But I just want to be with her."

"Yes, you want to be with the part of her that's fun and wild and great in bed and filled with laughter. But do you want to be with the scared little girl who uses drugs and alcohol to self-medicate? Because she's that person, too."

"But that's not who she really is," Alan protested. "She's this incredible person once you get rid of all that stuff."

"But, Alan, so is everybody," I said. "Everybody is this incredibly verdant field. But 'that stuff' is part of her as well. It's not separate. It's like saying the brick wall is not part of the open field. But it is. You've got to learn to love the brick wall as well. That's what love is—not just loving the parts that are fun, sexy, and creative—but seeing and loving the other parts as well. And allowing them."

We talked about it for a long time. It is not a loving act to try to get somebody to be ready who is not, even if they are the right person. And it never works because *the right person at the wrong time is the wrong person.*

Six months later, Alan and Suzie ran into each other in a restaurant; all the old chemistry was there. They had a long conversation and Suzie asked Alan to wait six more months. Instead of protesting and trying to get her to change, to be ready now, he respected her request. He accepted this as reality that was immutable, and said that he wanted to support her sobriety.

Six months later they started their relationship. Suzie was sober and so was Alan. While the wild ride was still there, with all its passion, they were now able to have a sober relationship, one based on trust, honesty, and a deeper understanding of who they each were.

She had asked for time, and Alan had given it to her. She cleared up what she needed to, and in doing so she learned to trust herself and to trust Alan, who had shown himself to be loving, accepting her boundaries.

It seemed as if it was going to work out, but then Alan showed up at my house a second time.

"She's gone again," Alan said. "I did everything you said, and she's gone again. Everything seemed to be amazing."

"But, Alan, this is who she is—she's an addict, and not just to alcohol. It sounds like she is a person who is addicted to the infatuation stage of relationship. As soon as the falling-in-love 'high' wears off, she starts to feel internal conflict. Love for her equals pain, she can't hang with it."

"I don't know which to believe," Alan said. "One day she's pledging her undying love, the next she's saying it's over."

"The only thing to do is to love her anyway, without conditions," I said. "You are on the roller coaster, and the only thing to do is stay seated. You will be riding the ups and downs as long as you choose to be with her. She will always be trying to jump out of her seat because love makes her feel uncomfortable. But that doesn't mean she doesn't love you and that you can't still love her, accept her, and accept this part of her. It can be a meaningful spiritual path, as long as you don't expect her to be consistent."

"A lesson in impermanence?" Alan said, smiling.

"Exactly," I said. "This is who she is, along with all the rest of her. Life will always change with her. The relationship will always feel impermanent with her."

Alan may go back many times to Suzie, who may flee

again and again. It just may be their dynamic. By doing this instead of getting mad and saying "Don't ever darken my doorstep again," the charge will dissipate. Trying to deny the connection may just keep it alive. The opposite of love isn't hate, it's indifference. Eventually Alan and Suzie may stick together or they may never, ending up with that puzzled and indifferent feeling of "Why him?" or "Why her?" But either way, change is inevitable. Allow it to happen because fighting it is like trying to hold water in your cupped hands. It's impossible, it will eventually leak out.

And understand the flip side of this axiom: Forcing somebody to change is impossible.

And unloving.

And the quickest way to lose your own internal freedom.

Don't trade your freedom for anything.

# PAYING ATTENTION

## Watering the Flower of Partnership

Love is or it ain't.
Thin love ain't love at all.

TONI MORRISON

"I know he loves me, but sometimes I feel like he wouldn't notice if I died unless he ran out of clean underwear," Marcy said, only half joking. "Is this what happens after you've been married fourteen years, both of us over-worked, with two kids? I'm only forty and I feel eighty."

Marcy has hit on something that we in America don't even recognize, it's so much a part of our lives. We are all overworked. We work much harder than anybody in the world (even the plumbers in Europe get six weeks of paid vacation) and most people are working hard just trying to hold it all together. In *City Dharma,* I devoted a lot of time to the general drift of our nation toward more hours for less pay, and to the growing chasm between the wealthy and the disappearing middle class. I talked about how most people are feeling burnt out, at home, at work, in their lives. And recent studies have shown what we have long suspected, that women are doing far more of the work at home, in addition to holding down full-time jobs.

The main thing about being in any relationship is that your partner wants to be seen and heard. This sounds so simple as to be obvious, but it is one of the most difficult things to do.

Giving your partner your full attention is a gift. And no matter what our advertising society may say about purchasing gifts, at the end of the day, nothing means more than your simple presence. It is so easy, after years have passed, to treat your partner like the wallpaper, always there, not going anywhere, perhaps not even that interesting.

In short, it is easy to take each other for granted, until the relationship codifies and we stagnate.

It's ironic that when we first meet our beloved we are so infatuated that we want to know every last thing about them. Of course, we don't usually see them clearly then, but only our projection of them. But at least we want to know all about them. Then we think we do, so we begin listening with half an ear. Soon there is no intimacy at all and it gets boring. One person checks out completely or has an affair or files for divorce.

So how do you combat this form of checking out?

This book is not about spicing up your marriage life or "getting the sex you deserve." There are plenty of lifestyle magazines that will cover that topic in its endless permutations.

This book, if it is about anything, is about the simple act of being fully present and awake in the moment. This means being awake to whatever aspect of reality is presenting itself.

In short, it means simply paying attention.

Right now, as you read these words, it means *only reading these words,* one by one.

As you drive your car, it means paying attention, *driving your car.*

And when you sit with your partner at your thousandth dinner, you really pay attention to them. You notice what they say and how they are saying it, as well as what they don't say. You tune in to their body language and their nonverbal communication, such as sighs or facial gestures. You are very present. Awake. Giving them the most important gift you can give them, your time and your careful attention.

Simply listening can become a form of meditation, even if you are listening to the same thing over and over—in fact, *especially* if you are listening to the same thing over and over again. It is a wonderful way to drop your own small self and story of me, me, me; you get to merge your awareness with another human being and become free from your small self. It does not get more interesting than that!

Simply be with what is.

And like a flower that is given water and flourishes, allow your attention to be the water for your partner. Pour this attention upon your partner and watch them flourish, much in the same way reality grows more intense and more beautiful the more you pour your attention into it. Your attention can be careful listening, small gestures, or even simple eye contact.

Out of this is born intimacy.

When we are being intimate, there can be no boredom.

# FORGIVENESS

## Cornerstone of Love

Forgiveness is an embrace, across all barriers,
against all odds, in defiance of all that is mean and
petty and vindictive and cruel in this life.

KENT NERBURN

When your partner disappoints you—and he or she will, in ways large and small—how do you live with it? How do you let go of some behavior that is so egregious, so horrible, that it feels as if it has wounded you to the bottom of your soul? How do you stay with them after that?

Well, the answer is, maybe you stay with them, maybe you don't. I don't advocate either path. Sometimes staying with a person is not the path to personal spiritual growth, even though it honors wedding vows. And sometimes leaving a person is the best thing for your spiritual growth. And vice versa. If you're afraid of commitment and intimacy, then staying in a relationship might be more fruitful. If you're afraid of independence and are treated like a doormat in all aspects of your life, then leaving might be the best thing to do. There are no "shoulds."

But either way, at the end of the day, it is best to get to some kind of forgiveness in order to move on, either in the relationship or out of it. Even if you break it off with them and never see them again, forgiving them will allow you to release your ties with the person, both literally and energetically. Not energetically in the sense that there is some kind of invisible force field between the two of you, but in the sense that they are not eating up the present moment of your life. You are not consumed by feelings of anger or fantasies of revenge. You can be present and alive without living in the past.

The precursor to forgiveness is acceptance, seeing others as they really are at the heart of their limitations as human beings. Before this comes self-acceptance, seeing who *you are,* in all your humanness. Accepting your limitations with compassion and not beating yourself up for your flaws, perceived and otherwise, is necessary in order to get to compassion for others. It is necessary in order to drop your story, cutting the self-recriminating tape in your own head that was implanted as a result of your own conditioning.

The thoughts come and come: *"I'm a failure," "I wish I was smarter or better looking,"* or *"If I had that girl, then I could be happy."*

They are not you.

You are not your thoughts.

If you are not your thoughts, then what are you?

You are the awareness from which the thoughts arise.

The thoughts themselves are just a matter of conditioning. As I've said before, your mind is a product of a combination of nature (genetic predisposition) and nurture (environmental conditioning). The nature is the biological hard-wiring of genetics and DNA. The nurture is the software of family, environment, and culture. All of it is an accident of birth.

So the tape that is running in your head, the one that says you're not good enough or whatever, is simply an accident of birth. Get born into a judgmental family, get low self-esteem. Get born into a loving family, feel good about yourself. The thoughts arise out of the conditioning, and they are relentless. Either way, they are not who you really are.

So, how do you deal with that tape? Well, some spiritual programs say you should stop it completely using any number of techniques, from meditation to chanting to trance dancing. These are all fine in themselves. Do them if you enjoy them. But notice that when you stop the technique, the thoughts come flooding in again. The technique is only a pause button for the incessant chatter of your mind. Then you are stuck with a sense of frustration that you have failed in your spiritual assignment. You are not progressing, your mind is getting the better of you; you haven't been able to still it.

Another way people try to deal with that tape is to change it so that it is positive. Think only positive thoughts, try to "manifest your reality" through what you think. There are entire programs, either through "channelers" bringing secret teachings or shamans promising to unveil the inner workings of the universe, that promise to teach you how to control what happens to you. But this, too, usually ends in frustration, either because it's too hard, or because it doesn't work. Reality, in my direct experience, doesn't conform to my thoughts. It has an objective innateness all of its own. In other words, the universe is neither negative nor positive, but largely neutral.

There is another aspect to this: control. Most forms of spirituality and religion promise some control over life and death as a result of believing in their doctrines. Believe this and you will go to heaven, believe that and you will go to hell. Act this way and you will be reincarnated in a higher form, act that way and you will come back as a frog. All this is about control, controlling your destiny after you die and controlling your destiny here and now.

But there is no such thing as control.

Control is an illusion with which we comfort ourselves. But the bottom line is that we have no idea what the next moment will bring. We like to tell ourselves that the next moment will bring this or that, but we don't know for sure.

This is the heart of being a mystic. It is in accepting the mysterious nature of life, becoming very comfortable with the ambiguity and lack of control in life, that one attains freedom. There is no freedom in trying to control reality or thoughts or people or anything else. For then you are tied to an outcome. You are not free; your sense of well-being and happiness depends on the actions of other people. You develop, in current psychological parlance, a codependent relationship with the rest of the world.

True freedom means not depending upon anything outside of you, because there is no *you* to whom anything is happening.

So you are not tied to a belief. The Anglo-Saxon definition of *belief* is "a wishing." It is a wishing that if a certain thing happens then I will be happy. It is the heart of the if-then way of being in the world. *If* this happens, *then* I can be happy. In other words, it is allowing the mind to make deals with itself in order to control reality. But if you do engage in that dynamic, it never ends. The next thing happens and it is unsatisfying or not enough or whatever. You then set another goal for yourself, after which you can then become happy. And so it goes. But happiness is the way, not the goal. Be happy NOW, for it is the only time you can be happy.

So, what is the best way to deal with these conditioned thoughts? How do you get to have compassion for them? You get there by simply ignoring them. Let them burble along in the background, like a stream as you go hiking in a forest. Present, constant, louder sometimes as you pay attention to it, softer sometimes as you bring your attention to the present moment.

Just let the thoughts be. Accept that they are a part of your conditioning, and learn to have compassion for them. Have compassion for yourself and the experiences that might have created them. In short, forgive yourself for having these thoughts. It is only then that you can forgive those who hurt you and were instrumental in creating the thoughts in the first place. And in forgiving those who first wounded you, you can forgive those who wound you now.

Once you can accept and forgive yourself, then the dynamic of compassion is in play. It is only then that you can move on to accepting others, even those who have mistreated you. You can accept who they are, and in doing so, eventually you can forgive them for what they've done. You have no belief that they should be any other way than the way they are.

It is in forgiveness that you can drop the story of what

happened in the past. You can come out of the twilight of imagination. It is through forgiveness that you become free to deal with what is right now.

The alternative is to be in constant war, either personally or on the level of nations. It is the difference between Nelson Mandela's formula of forgiveness through an honest airing of atrocities committed by both sides during the Truth and Reconciliation trials and a potentially endless war of retribution and genocide, like what happened in Rwanda.

And so it can be between two people. For if you don't learn to forgive, you are tied to the other person; you can never really cut the bond. This is not to say you need to do it before you are ready, or that other emotions such as anger and depression don't need to be worked through first.

But in the end, it is forgiveness that will set you free.

# COMPASSION

## The Highest Form of Love

The mind will take you into the courtyard of
the Beloved, but only the heart will
get you into the bedroom.

RAMAKRISHNA

"You know, I think something in me has shifted," I said to a
close friend. "In almost every relationship I'm in, I'm finding myself giving love in the form of compassion. Sarah,
Patty, and Julia, all of them are in tough spots right now
and I find I can really show up without agenda. I feel compassion for them."

"Good," my friend said. "Next you'll be able to show up
for, fat, ugly, bald guys in the same way, instead of all your
hot female friends."

"That's not fair!" I protested. "I just got a message from
a very bald friend who called me an angel for helping him
out."

"What did you do?"

"I was on my way to a lunch and I got a call from him. He was three hours away up the coast and he had just gotten a message from his dog sitter that his beloved dog was dying. Oscar had woken up and hadn't moved all day and the woman, a new dog sitter, wouldn't take her to the vet."

"What?!" My friend, a dog lover, was furious. "Why not?"

"She said Oscar was dying and nature had to take its course. Now, this is a dog that is on a lot of meds, so she had no right to make that decision—who knows what was wrong? So my friend was frantic. He asked me to pick up Oscar and take him to his vet, who was familiar with Oscar's history."

"What happened?"

"I had already said to him that if anything happened with Oscar, he should call me. I've been alone when a pet dies, and it is the worst feeling in the world. So I was at the woman's house in ten minutes flat."

"What was she like?"

"Very strange energy, like . . . you know, one of these people who probably hangs out a lot with animals because she has no people skills. She had Oscar lying on a blanket in the driveway, and the poor dog couldn't even lift his head. I asked her a couple of quick medical questions and then loaded Oscar into my car. It's about a half-hour drive and I thought Oscar was going to die in my car—eyes rolling back in his head, heavy panting."

"Jesus."

"Anyway, none of this is the point of the story. I was in contact with my friend the whole time, and I stayed with Oscar at the vet's until he came in with a few other friends three hours later. The vet, in an incredibly kind way, said that Oscar had probably suffered a blood clot from the Cushing's disease he had, and would probably die within twenty-four hours. My friend made the decision to bring Oscar home and, if he hadn't died by morning, to put him to sleep. He died at home the next day. When my friend called me, he thanked me profusely. He called me an angel who'd gone in and done a kind of military extraction of Oscar."

"Okay, okay, maybe you are compassionate after all."

"No. That's not the point. When I said to Nate that I was honored to do it and that I couldn't have done anything else, he said, 'That's because you're such a good friend.' But that wasn't it. I mean, I am a good friend. But I simply couldn't have acted any other way. And not just for a friend, but for *anybody* in that circumstance. I didn't *do* anything."

"So what's your point?" My friend was looking at me fish-eyed.

"My point is that that is what compassion is. It is not a doing. It is when *you can't do otherwise,* when it becomes part of you. You don't try to be compassionate, you simply drop the story that you're not. I even felt that way for the dog sitter who was acting so strangely. I could see that she was just freaked out and completely couldn't handle the fact that the dog was dying. I couldn't even build up a case for judging her. In fact, letting go of judgment in that moment allowed me to be compassionate. It also allowed me to be effective, to get Oscar out of there."

"But if you're saying that compassion is when you can't do anything else, it's almost like you're saying that you're not the one being compassionate. You're not *doing anything.*"

"Exactly. Exactly right. In the moment of being compassionate, there is no sense of 'look at me being so compassionate.' If that's there, then its just ego gratification. It's more like compassion arises of its own accord. It's almost like breathing. You're not really thinking about breathing, you are just *being breathed*. I mean, who or what is doing the breathing? Who or what is being compassionate?"

"Okay, okay. Maybe you are compassionate."

We laughed and then walked in silence for a while, contemplating it.

When you are compassionate, there is no thinking, no sense of "I" or "me." There is just a doing and a feeling—an empathetic sense of same-same with other people. Under all the conditioning we receive to be individualistic, to achieve something for ourselves, to be competitive in the world and to "get our own," lies a sweet sense of compassion.

The ability to put yourself in another's shoes and, in doing so, lose your identification with the small self, with all the sense of entitlement and self-absorption that leaves us all so isolated and lonely, is a relief. In the lack of identification with self, you become more sensitive to, and compassionate with, what is happening with other people, whether they are your lover or a perfect stranger.

Compassion is the highest form of love because you are not getting the "high" associated with romantic love or the support that comes with love of friends and family. There is no quid pro quo.

You are able to show up and be loving.

It is also our true nature. Yes—in everybody.

My friend Louise told me a story of the time she was traveling to Seattle and was staying at a hotel where there was a national conference for blind people. As she was preparing to leave, she heard a blind woman say to a hotel employee that she was catching the eleven-thirty flight to San Francisco. When my friend realized it was the same flight she was taking, she offered her services to the woman. They rode to the airport together and my friend helped her get through security, onto the plane, and into her seat.

When they flew into the airport at Oakland, they hooked up again and my friend helped the woman down the stairs and onto the tarmac. This is when she realized something extraordinary.

The plane was full of blind people, all of whom had spontaneously hooked up with impromptu escorts. The tarmac was filled with people with canes, and every one had a hand on the shoulder of another person, who was guiding them. And the thing my friend said is that the escorts came in all shapes and sizes. Some were unlikely, like the biker dude with long hair and a tattoo or the woman wearing nose rings and low-cut jeans. Or a teenager who was doing her best impersonation of "Paris Hilton meets Britney Spears."

My friend had this *moment*. She saw all the compassion on display, coming from different kinds of people, and she realized we were all capable of it when presented with the right opportunity. A person or animal in dire need naturally brings out an impulse to help. When, through the power of being very present and aware in this moment, right now, you awaken to your true nature as consciousness, your heart opens. Then kindness, love, and generosity become the natural cornerstones of your behavior.

Magrabi Sahib, a spiritual master from India, said this: "When I looked in, I found within me that which has been sought for ages by all mankind. We have been searching for it for many ages here and there, from one corner of the earth to the other, but we have found it only in our heart. Therefore do not search for your lost Beloved outside yourself. You will find Him—or Her—only in the recess of your heart."

Because this love and compassion, underneath our striving and competitive nature, is what we really are.

# PART FIVE

# The End

## When It's Over

# GETTING "DUMPED"

## Rejection Is Protection

*Reality is that which, when you stop believing in it, doesn't go away.*

PHILIP K. DICK

Getting rejected at any stage of a relationship can be incredibly painful and trigger conditioning in us that is so dormant it can sometimes take us completely by surprise. Often it doesn't seem to matter to what level the relationship has progressed. The guy you've been dating for two months who pulls the plug can feel as bad as the end of a four-year marriage. It also doesn't seem to matter if the reason the relationship ended is perfectly justified.

For example, Bill dated Laura for a few months. They had just progressed to the stage where they had slept together for the first time. Before they slept together, Bill had made a big deal about never ejaculating when he had sex. It wasn't that he was a Tantric sex practitioner, where the orgasm in the male is controlled and redirected, resulting in profound, "all-body" waves of orgasm. Bill just never came. While Laura thought this was a bit strange and controlling, she also thought: *Whatever works for you, as long as you don't impose the same on me!*

Oddly, when they made love, Bill ended up having the opposite problem; he suffered from an immediate premature ejaculation. Bill mumbled how this had never happened to him before. Two days later, in a casual conversation Bill said that he would probably date other people if he met somebody more attractive to him. Laura immediately pulled the plug on the relationship—who wants to go out with somebody who's going to do that?

Laura, who had previously been in a long and emotionally brutal relationship, was in no mood to place herself in an unsafe situation again. She cut all contact with Bill, who reacted with surprising behavior for somebody who was treating the relationship so casually. He showed up at her house unannounced and in tears. He called her repeatedly, even after Laura had requested him not to. He was incredibly remorseful and wanted to try again. He was terribly hurt and upset that she would cut contact, even though it was he who wanted to keep it all casual.

What could account for such behavior in somebody who professed such a casual connection with Laura that he would leave her as soon as somebody better came along? Perhaps he was embarrassed by his sexual performance and was unconsciously trying to create distance with his comment. Maybe he didn't really feel casual about her. Or he didn't know that he actually had strong feelings for her. But perhaps it was simply getting rejected that triggered him. In spite of his odd behavior, he was devastated by her rejection.

Why?

Recent research has shown that a rejected lover's broken heart may cause as much distress in a pain center of the brain as an actual physical injury. By monitoring the brains of people who thought they had been maliciously excluded from a computer game by other players, California researchers have found a physiological basis for social pain. Naomi I. Eisenberger, a scientist at the University of California, Los Angeles, in a study published in the journal *Science,* wrote that results suggest that the need for social inclusiveness is a deep-seated part of what it means to be human.

"These findings show how deeply rooted our need is for social connection," said Eisenberger. "There's something about exclusion from others that is perceived as being as harmful to our survival as something that can physically hurt us, and our body automatically knows this."

The shock and distress of this rejection registered in the same part of the brain, called the anterior cingulate cortex, that also responds to physical pain.

"The ACC is the same part of the brain that has been found to be associated with the unpleasantness of physical pain, the part of pain that really bothers us," Eisenberger reported.

The study suggests that social exclusion of any sort—divorce, not being invited to a party, being turned down for a date—causes distress in the ACC.

"You can imagine that this part of the brain is active anytime we are separated from our close companions," Eisenberger said. "It would definitely be active when we experience a loss, such as a death or the end of a love affair."

So Bill, in addition to whatever conditioning he had around the issue of abandonment, was also at the mercy of universal human biology.

But what really happens when we are rejected by a lover? Of course, any kind of rejection can hurt. But when somebody breaks up with you, they are saying, for reasons real or imagined, that *they can't be with you*. They don't *get you*. They aren't in harmony with *who you are*.

It is extremely important to really listen to somebody who says this to you.

My inclination in this situation used to be to try to persuade the person: "What do you mean? We have so much in common. Our sex life is so great. I love you so much. I just know we're meant to be together! You're just feeling some fear coming up," et cetera ad nauseam. If I wasn't the one who wanted the relationship to end, I would try to save it. This never worked, not even once. There are many things one can say about this, but it boils down to the principle of acceptance. Seeing the other person clearly and accepting where they are is the only loving thing to do, even when they are walking out the door. Anything else, especially trying to change the emotional states of others, falls into the sinkhole of manipulation. Sometimes it is a mystery and must be accepted as such.

Try to love them whether they are walking toward you or walking away.

When Laura rejected Bill, for very specific and, in her mind, obvious reasons, his subsequent actions, while all too human, belied a profound lack of understanding of what had just happened. He accessed some deeper part of himself and realized that he had fallen in love with her (at least his version of it). He did care. He didn't want to date other people. He did want to try. But she didn't see that. She didn't see the shift in him. Or she saw it and it seemed desperate and too soon. She moved on. He was devastated by it, and continued to call her even when she asked him not to.

The next person Laura dated was present, uncomplicated, and really liked her. There was attraction on both sides. Samuel was attentive and appreciated Laura on all levels. They spoke the same emotional language and had wide-ranging conversations. After a couple of months, in which there had been no progression in the dating—they had kissed once or twice—Laura rejected Samuel, saying that she "just couldn't do it."

"Do what?" Samuel asked.

"I just have too much on my plate right now emotionally. I don't feel . . . comfortable. I'm used to kind of all consuming relationships . . ." She faltered. "I guess I need to look at how prepared I am for a healthy relationship right now."

Samuel was disappointed. It was rare that he found somebody in whom he was interested. He wanted to argue his case, but knew the futility of doing so. He wished her well, thinking that he had lost out.

Two cases of rejection, both at the hands of the same woman, but for the opposite reasons. One man didn't want to commit. The other did. One melodramatically pursued Laura after she left. Samuel accepted things and left Laura to her process.

But both felt . . . *disappointed*.

What neither of them realized is that *rejection is protection*.

Protection from what? From the actions of somebody who does not see the light within you. Or they see it but can't meet it. Or they see it and feel inferior to it, not ready for it, unable to access a light within themselves that is of a similar wattage. Or they see you as you were a week ago, and not as you are now. For whatever reason, and it doesn't really matter what the reason, they simply don't want to be with you.

To put yourself in the way of such a person is like throwing yourself against a brick wall. It will only hurt you in the end. In fact, if you forget this, find the closest brick wall and lightly bang your hand against it. Yep. It's a brick wall and you are not going to change that. This is a useful reminder. You're not going to change a rock into a flower by the sheer force of your will.

But no matter what the biological programming that equates rejection with pain, on a deeper level, when we are rejected, we are actually being *spared suffering*—even when it appears that this rejection is *causing* suffering.

Think back on any relationship you've been in that ended, even when you were desperately in love and were the one being dumped. Ultimately, was the one who rejected you the right person for you? Did they see you clearly and love you deeply? Was the relationship based on kindness and compassion? Could they not wait to see you at the end of the day? Was it even fun, or were you the one holding it all together?

How many times have you been selling a relationship, holding it together, trying really hard, being overly generous, all the while hoping that the other person would meet you with their generosity? Did it *ever* work?

What happened when you stopped agreeing to the relationship's mutual collusion that you would do all the work and the other person would enjoy the ride as long as you were doing all the work? When you stopped, didn't that person jump ship as soon as possible? Or at least slide away?

And in the end, weren't you actually protected from them and their unavailability?

For Laura wasn't really available. First she chose somebody unavailable and rightfully left them when they couldn't show up, all the while telling anybody who would listen how unavailable he was, how she wanted a man who could really commit. Until she ran into one. And then *she* couldn't commit.

Both Bill and Samuel went through the same rejection with the same woman, but for different reasons.

But by being rejected, they were being *spared*.

# WHEN IT'S
# REALLY OVER

## Dealing with the Breakup

The cure for anything is salt water—
sweat, tears or the sea.

ISAK DINESEN

There is an anonymous saying: "If a relationship doesn't end well, then it doesn't end."

Everybody has been through the difficulties of being dumped. And if you haven't, then you're either thirteen or fantastic at pulling the trigger before you yourself get shot. Ending a relationship is never easy, for either the person who is ending it or the person who is being broken up with. If you are ending it, you may feel guilty and responsible for causing another person pain. You are also causing yourself pain, even if is the right decision. If you are being broken up with, then you have no control—a relationship is ending that you may not want to end.

So, either you are in control, causing two people pain, or you have no control and are in pain by yourself.

No wonder people don't know how to handle a breakup. They would rather go have an affair and then unconsciously let the other person find out, thus letting the other person "end" the relationship. Or they will simply walk out on a partner with no explanation whatsoever. Or a man will treat a wife like she was simply a girlfriend and hide his money overseas and fight her for every nickel earned in their partnership. Or a woman will treat her husband, the father of her children, like an ATM machine while battling a divorce.

So let's walk through what is really happening during a breakup and think about how to do it in a way that is compassionate. During a breakup, somebody is *transitioning* a relationship, from that of a lover to that of a friend or an enemy or a nonentity. This is a transition that can be excruciatingly painful and result in hurt feelings, obsession, vicious gossip, disease, and violence. Or it can be a way of seeing reality clearly or choosing freedom or growing up or accepting the person as they really are or tossing in the towel on a protracted power struggle.

In any case, it is a transition, and during all transitions, you must take care of the person to whom you are giving the bad news. Kindness and compassion are the only way to help the other person through it.

In the moment of breaking up with somebody, you must understand that you are a bearer of bad news. Their world has momentarily collapsed. They are numb or enraged or heartbroken. Your job is to be there with them and allow them the full range of their feelings, no matter how uncomfortable they may make you feel (short of abuse, of course). Don't try to control them. Don't try to console them. Just be there and be gentle but firm, carefully enunciating your reasons. Try to do it at a time when you're not angry.

The end of a relationship is like a death. In fact, it is sometimes worse than a death because there isn't the finality or lack of control that death provides. The other person isn't gone forever; they're living down the street, dating other people, and showing up at your gym or your yoga class. The stages of accepting death, including denial, anger, bargaining, depression, and acceptance, show up around any grief or the receipt of any catastrophic news.

The five stages of grief were defined by Elisabeth Kübler-Ross in her book *On Death and Dying* (Macmillan, 1969). There she presents the five stages terminally ill persons may go through after learning of terminal illness. She presents them as "an attempt to summarize what we have learned from our dying patients in terms of coping mechanisms at the time of a terminal illness." These stages were not originally the five stages of grief; they were "the five stages of receiving catastrophic news," which I actually like better. Another good working and practical definition of grief is "the total response of the organism to the process of change."

Grief is considered by some specialists as a kind of unified field theory for all mental illness; significant grief responses that go unresolved can lead to mental, physical, and sociological problems and contribute to family dysfunction across generations. One thing is clear, that Change = Loss = Grief. The intensity of the grief reaction is a function of how the change or loss is perceived. If the loss is not perceived as significant, the grief reaction will be minimal or barely felt.

So the five stages of receiving catastrophic news can produce a grief response around any event. In the arena of relationship, it might play out like this: you have received the news that your boyfriend or husband or wife is leaving you.

1.  **DENIAL:** What's the first thing you do? You try to talk him or her out of it! Again and again. You refuse to believe it's true. You continue calling them. This can't be happening; we were going to get married!

2.  **ANGER:** "%$@^##& you!" "Screw you and the horse you rode in on. You're the biggest jerk in the world. You've betrayed me!"

3.  **BARGAINING:** "Oh, please, let's give it one more try. I'm finally ready to go to counseling. I know we can work this out. If you give it one more try, I promise I'll never leave the toilet seat up again!"

4.  **DEPRESSION:** "Oh God, what am I going to do? I'm never going to find anybody to be with again. I'm so unlovable and I don't really care anymore. What's the use?"

5.  **ACCEPTANCE:** "Okay. It's over. Guess I had better get on with it, get back into my life. They're not coming back, but there are a lot of other people in the world."

We all go through this process numerous times a day, in ways both minor and major. A dead battery, the loss of a parking space, dropping a sandwich, the loss of a pet, a job, a move to another city, and so on. Here are some things to remember:

- Any change of circumstance can cause us to go through this process.
- We don't have to go through the stages in sequence. We can skip a stage or go through two or three simultaneously. It can be a "one step forward, two steps back" process.
- We can go through them in different time phases. The dead battery could take maybe five to ten minutes, dropping a sandwich five to ten seconds. A traumatic divorce that involves the criminal justice system can take years.
- The intensity and duration of the reaction depends on how significant the change or loss is perceived.

And you're not done there; grieving actually only begins where the five stages of "grief" leave off. Grief professionals often use the concept of "grief work" to help the bereaved through grief resolution. One common definition of grief work is summarized by the acronym TEAR:

T = To accept the reality of the loss
E = Experience the pain of the loss
A = Adjust to the new environment without the lost object
R = Reinvest in the new reality

This is grief work. It begins when the divorce is over, the friends have stopped calling, and everyone thinks you should be over it. "Closure" has been achieved, and everything is supposed to be back to normal. But it's at this point that real grieving begins. They are all necessary stages of grief to go through in the end of a relationship. They can't be rushed or skipped—the worst thing you can do for somebody in this situation is tell them to "cheer up."

I have a friend right now who is going through a divorce. She is completely heartbroken and in a kind of agonizing pain. She called me and said she'd spent the day crying so much that she literally couldn't see.

"This is good," I said.

"Easy for you to say," she said. "I just want it to end."

"It will end when it ends," I said. "On the other side of all these tears is wholeness and happiness. There's no way around it. Better to just accept this and be happy it's happening, because the sooner you get through it, the sooner you will again become your happy self."

Intense grief is like when you're going to throw up. There is all the anxiety and feeling bad and nausea of the soul. But just as when you get sick, after you purge, you feel better. There is no way around it. And when you're in the grieving process, there is nothing to do except treat it the same way as the flu. Be gentle with yourself and take time off with yourself. Don't expect to be the "good soldier," and be as productive as you were before. Don't expect it to be different, for the resistance will make it even worse and it just won't happen—you are down for the count, however long it takes.

Whether you are the heartbreaker or the heartbroken, you must accept these stages and allow them in the other person and equally important, allow them in yourself.

So know that whether you are inflicting a breakup or

receiving it, grief is going to be a large component of what is happening. When you're going through a separation, when you've decided that you have tried everything possible and it is time to call it quits, remember to treat the other person with compassion and tenderness. If you have learned everything you can by loving in this particular relationship, then you continue the loving behavior throughout the separation. Treading with compassion makes it easier on everybody.

How do you do this?

By remembering that love is within you and not dependent upon the person you are with. So you end the relationship, transitioning it with the same care you expressed when you were in it.

For, when a person is in your heart, and at one time they actually filled your heart, don't they deserve respect and care and love, even if you are not going to be together? We've all had partners who just split without an explanation or even a phone call or an e-mail. This makes it so much more difficult to get through it that it's tantamount to a kind of intentional cruelty. Sitting down face to face with your partner, patiently hearing them out and answering their questions, will make it so much easier for them to get over the denial of what is happening. This, in turn, will make it easier for you to move on.

Go through the separation without identifying with your ego needs—what the other did or didn't do.

Go through the separation with the understanding and the realization that your partner, whom you have chosen to learn with, is another manifestation of consciousness. You have chosen them to learn something spiritual.

Learn it.

In this awareness, any separation is only apparent, not real. They are not separate; they are a part of the one, as are you, connected by the love you felt and expressed, no matter what happened when it ended. Your love has left a stain in time; it will always be there.

Honor what you have had together by not hurting each other during the separation. Honor your personality's reactions and grief. Remember that you were fine before you met this partner and you will be fine after they are gone.

And then get very quiet.

In the stillness of the present moment, take a deep breath and let it all go.

And allow the possibilities of the NOW to dance into your awareness.

Who knows what this moment might bring?

# OBSESSION

## Snap Out of It!

*Every sweet has its sour; every evil its good.*

RALPH WALDO EMERSON

Sarah is a beautiful woman in her mid-thirties. A successful interior decorator with a mane of red hair, she is constantly in demand from her wealthy clients who buy and sell houses all the time. Her work and her looks also bring her into contact with a lot of celebrities, some of whom are single or recently divorced. One day a well-known actor asked her out. He was twenty years older, in his mid-fifties. They went out to an expensive restaurant and he was charming and effusive—and he admitted that his longest relation-ship to date was three months. He just hadn't found the right person (!). After going back to his house, he appeared drunk, even though they hadn't drunk that much. His speech was slurred and he was bumping into walls. Still, they began fooling around. In the middle of making out, the man,

whom I'll call Ricky, took out his penis and began mastur-
bating. Sarah was so shocked that she didn't say anything as,
a moment later, Ricky ejaculated on her.

And while this story should have been the end of the
relationship—what else is there to say when a celebrity
treats you like an object, uses you like a human tissue?—it
wasn't. Sarah and Ricky developed a relationship. Or at
least she thought that's what she was doing. Her guts were
telling her something else was going on. Maybe it was the
candle she bought for her new lover's bedroom, which,
when she saw it a couple of nights later, had been lit, perhaps to illuminate another woman. But she ignored this and
several other clues. She even managed to suppress the de-
tails of their first date.

Sounds like "the end is in the beginning," right? But,
blinded by celebrity and gifts and A-list parties and pre-
mieres, Sarah ignored her instincts and the nagging doubts
in her head. And Ricky assured her how much he cared for
her and how special she was.

After six months, Sarah found out the truth, that Ricky
had been dating other women the entire time they were
supposed to be in a monogamous relationship. Sex for a
male celebrity in our celebrity-crazed culture is as available
as leaves on a tree—it's just a matter of picking and choosing. All the signs were there for Sarah to see, but she just
couldn't tell the truth to herself faster.

As she was breaking up with Ricky, Sarah's phone began
to make funny static noises. Ricky began tossing out phrases
and letting slip certain things about her that she hadn't told
him directly, but that she had mentioned by phone to a
close friend. Her antenna was missing from her car for a
couple of days and then put back on. She became convinced

that Ricky, worried about what she might say about him in public, was tapping her phones and having her followed.

During this time I became close friends with Sarah, who seemed increasingly isolated. She couldn't stop talking about what was going on in her life, how weird everything was, what with strange vans following her and cable repairmen showing up without any identification on them. Every single conversation was spent totally and obsessively on what Ricky was doing, what he had done.

One night she burst into tears. We were on the couch and I began holding her. She seemed on the verge of a nervous breakdown and she started touching me. She touched my chest and stomach and thighs, even brushing up against my groin. At first I thought she was, in her grief, making a pass, trying to forget everything. But then I realized that it was something else entirely.

"What are you doing?" I asked.

"Nothing. I'm . . ."

"Did you just frisk me?" I said. "Did you just pat me down? You think I'm wearing a wire? Spying on you for Ricky?"

"Well, everything is just so weird. I don't know. I don't know anything anymore."

"Sarah. I'm on your side. Something is obviously happening. I don't doubt that Ricky might be tapping your phones. It happens all the time. But you have no reason to pat me down—you know what kind of person I am."

"I know. I know. I'm just confused. I'm just . . ."

"Obsessed. For the past two months it's the only thing you've talked about."

"I know, but it's so strange. It's all been so strange. When is it going to end?"

I looked deeply into her troubled brown eyes.

"It's going to end when it ends in here," I said, tapping her lightly on the forehead.

"But real things have been happening."

"I believe you. But right now you are frisking a close friend. You've crossed the line here. It's also the only thing, without exception, that you've been talking about for six weeks. Your mind has got you in a vise. There is a whole world out there."

Sarah nodded.

"But Ricky . . ."

"Ricky? Ricky has moved on. Right now Ricky is shooting his next movie, screwing his next three-month 'relationship,' and not giving you a second thought except maybe to be glad you haven't gone to the *National Enquirer* about the size of his penis."

"It's small," Sarah said. We both cracked up laughing.

"Of course it is. Why else would he be such a misogynist?"

We stared at each other.

"I'm sorry for frisking you." It sounded so absurd that we started laughing again until we finally ran out of gas.

"Listen," I said. "I've been where you are. I've been obsessed. I've gone for weeks thinking about one thing, one person who abandoned me, who lied to me. It's understandable. But it hijacks your life. It drains you of everything else important. It prevents you from being present in the moment."

"I know, but how do I get out of it? How?"

"Your portal out of it is this very moment. Use it to pull yourself into your five senses. When your mind wanders into paranoid obsession, bring your attention to what you are tasting, touching, seeing, smelling, or hearing. Allow your senses to soak your awareness in right now. The horrible nightmare of your mind will disappear like a fog being burned off in sunlight."

Sarah slowly nodded.

"Sarah, the obsessive thoughts can't exist in the intensity of the NOW. It's impossible. Every time they come up, simply steer your attention into right now."

"Yeah . . ." Her voice trailed off, unconvinced.

"So do it. Right now. Waking up isn't something you can do in the future. It's impossible. So do it right now. Look at me. Hear my voice. Smell the flowers on the table. Do you hear the bird outside the window? Right now is the only time you can wake up."

We sat like that for a moment, then her face crumpled.

"But . . . I feel sad about it. Really sad."

"Yes. But that's just the point. Obsession has an addictive quality. It is like a drug we use to keep from feeling what we need to feel, which in your case is grief. I mean, you were promised love, you then had that love betrayed in the most callous way by somebody who just moved on. It hurts."

Sarah nodded again, her eyes filling with tears.

"Just feel the grief. On the other side of it is freedom. All that obsession is just delaying the inevitable."

A few days later, Sarah and I got together and we had our first conversation in months in which she didn't mention Ricky's name, not even once. It took a while, but using the present moment, Sarah was able to pull herself out of the downward spiral.

The mind will take you for the worst funhouse ride if you let it. As long as you believe it to be true, you will feel like you won't be able to get off. You will be screaming and puking and in misery, wondering if it will ever end. But the second you can, in the NOW, stop believing the thoughts to be true, the ride stops. You can breathe again. You can feel what you need to feel.

You are back in the land of the living.

# DIVORCE

## End of a Marriage or
## Beginning of a Friendship?

When I meet a man I ask myself, "Is this the man I want
my children to spend their weekends with?"

RITA RUDNER

There is nothing more difficult than the end of a marriage.
Perhaps death, but, as I've said before, divorce is a death
without the finality. It just keeps on going, dripping pain
like an IV. And the deeper the connection and the marriage,
the greater the passion and love, the deeper the anger and
disappointment when it ends. There's a fine line between
love and hate.

So how do you keep from crossing over that line when
you find yourself at the point of "irreconcilable differences"
and fighting over the house, the dog, and the CD collection?

Whole books have been written on conscious divorce:

how to negotiate a settlement, how to work out the separation of property and child custody issues. If Tolstoy was right that every family is happy in the same way, but miserable in their own specific way (and I think it's just the opposite), then every marriage is happy in the same way and every divorce is miserable in its own unique way. So many variables come into play: whether there are children, whether both couples worked, who made more money, how long the marriage lasted, whether another person is involved in the breakup.

Obviously I can't cover everything here in a short chapter. Nor have I been divorced, so my level of direct experience here is limited. But I have been involved in some hellacious breakups filled with all sorts of bad behavior, some of it my own. And I have witnessed divorce up close with several friends.

If there is one point that I want to make about divorce, it's this:

At some point you were absolutely, madly, deeply enough in love with your partner to say "I love you, I want to spend my life with you, until death do us part." You meant it in the most serious way, from the bottom of your heart.

Even if this vow gets shredded completely in the divorce, keep it in mind. You loved them. Treat them with dignity and respect. Try to be generous. Try to be communicative. Don't end it badly by disappearing from the process of closure. It is a tremendous kindness and can greatly help your wife or husband in their healing. You loved them and even if you are suffering from the loss, don't go out of your way to make them suffer. If you are a man with a lot of money, be generous. If you are a woman, don't use the children as a pawn.

One story of a divorce that I admire is that of Howard Stern. It may be true or it may be apocryphal, but either way it is a laudable example of a way to handle a divorce. When he talks about his divorce, he talks about his wife as the mother of his children. She was the woman who stood by him when he was nobody. Now he is a famous multimillionaire. Did he get a high-priced lawyer to fight for every cent? No. He sat down with his wife with a pencil and a piece of paper and handed it to her. I don't want to give a dime to lawyers, he said. I don't want to have any problem with you or the children. Write down a number. Be in the realm of reasonable and fair and I will give it to you. End of story.

She did, and that was that.

Is this story true? Maybe, maybe not. But if it is, it is an inspired way to handle a divorce.

I have another friend who almost got a divorce because her husband met another woman. He left her completely and suddenly, saying he had fallen in love. She was devastated, but never said a bad word about him. Even as the divorce was initiated and he was flying his new girlfriend to Hawaii, she remained gracious, not resisting it, not making him wrong. She gave him all the freedom he could have asked for to explore the relationship. After six months it ended; he realized it was all a dream, and he missed his wife and came back to her. They are together now. But even if it hadn't happened this way, even if he had left her for good, her response was right on. Love is not a prison or a contract. People are free to come and go.

This society has a completely immature idea of what marriage is, drawn mostly from Cinderella myths and Hollywood romantic comedies. All our attention is on the courtship phase. I want to see a Hollywood movie about what happens after the fade-out.

Unfortunately, a lot of people get married because they feel they've reached an age when they feel they should be married. They end up married before they are ready, and to people they don't really know. The marriage becomes a way in which they learn about who the other person is—and then they find out they don't even like them!

The end of a marriage is a huge opportunity to become more of who you really are at the core. It burns off the conditioning that drove you into a marriage in the first place, whether it was before you were ready or to the wrong person. Ending a union based on a former blindness is a transformational opportunity. You get the opportunity to wake up. You go through the most horrible pain and suffering, but according to many people I've spoken to, they wouldn't want to trade who they are now after the divorce with who they were before. Like a caterpillar becoming a butterfly, the struggle to grow out of the cocoon has made them stronger and more beautiful people. But not before the cocoon was liquified and they essentially became caterpillar soup. It was painful and traumatic, but they are now awake.

Eventually, it is also an opportunity to transform your relationship with your spouse. This is the person you loved enough to marry. Initially you may feel as if you never want to see them again. But don't they know you well? Haven't you expended a lot of energy getting to know them? Haven't they seen you at your worst? Couldn't the relationship eventually find equilibrium, transforming into a friendship?

Not all will. At some point you may just have grown so far apart that you never want to see your former spouse again. You have nothing in common. When you see them on the street, it is like looking through the wrong end of a telescope; they seem distant and small. Whether through different interests, paths, education, or level of interest in the marriage itself, in maintaining the intimacy in it, two people end up in different places. It's a bit like two space-ships traveling together in what seem like parallel courses, traveling in the same direction. But if the courses of those two ships deviate by a minuscule amount, over time they will end up in *different galaxies.*

Sometimes it's possible to transform yourself and transition your relationship into a friendship. And if there are children involved, you have no choice. You must make this transition. You cannot poison the children's view of their mother or father, for even when you get divorced, your ex-spouse is still their parent, whether or not you hate them.

But if you do end up in different galaxies, what then?

Well, rather than seeing it as the end of the world, understand that a huge part of the pain you are feeling is not just the end of the marriage. It is the end of the dream of *happily ever after.* The end of a dream of a certain way of life.

But, dream or not, it is still a heartbreak. It is so painful and there is so much suffering at the end of a marriage because it burns off all the romantic illusions. It is a kind of suffering that leads to spiritual growth—you will see reality more clearly at the end of the process, at which point you might look at your partner in the cold light of day and say, "What was I thinking?"

Use the suffering to go inside. Be like a phoenix rising from the ashes. The mountain of suffering will help you burn off your illusions and see through them. Going through a divorce gives you the chance to see people clearly for who they are and perhaps love them anyway.

Start with yourself. The suffering will create compassion in yourself if you engage it correctly; that's what the suffering is for, to break down the ego, to soften you up. At the beginning, the middle, and the end of it, you have the absolute freedom that the present moment supplies—every moment gives you an opportunity for love—with friends, strangers, relatives, and animals.

The first law of thermodynamics in physics says that energy is neither created nor destroyed, but it does change forms. The same could be said for love. The love that you felt for your spouse wasn't created by them and can't be destroyed by them, but you can transform it. You can use the pain and sorrow and loss to find a deeper understanding of love, one that reverses the flow of "what can I get" to "what can I give." In this way we can grow beyond our identification with our small self and all of our needs. We can grow to become giants of love.

So be in love with the world, even as you are contracted down in your pain. Know that your pain is part of your spiritual growth and transformation. It is not negative or bad. It will temper you and free you from the tightness of your conditioning. It is making you more human and humane.

On the other side of the suffering is freedom and a more spacious way of being in the world.

On the other side the butterfly of your true self awaits you.

# IMPERMANENCE

## What Comes Around Goes Away

*Oh, this is the joy of the rose:*
*That it blows,*
*And goes.*

WILLA CATHER

A friend of mine was once in an on-again-off-again relationship with a girlfriend for three years. They fell in love with each other, shared similar interests in music, were both bookworms, and loved nature. They had insane sexual chemistry and were positively giddy around each other.

When they met, Megan was coming out of a relationship, which turned out to be not quite over, and they lasted six months before she went back to her ex-boyfriend. The next time they met, she had again ended that relationship, but was still in the throes of letting it go—so they went back and forth for a month. The third time they saw each other, she had been single for a year. She was working deeply

on herself and said she wasn't ready to be in a relationship. She needed more time to learn to be in a relationship
with herself. Having learned his lesson, my friend Tom
didn't argue. He accepted what was, and said they would
meet again when were both ready.

A couple of weeks ago they connected again. Tom has
given me the blow-by-blow—how they still had all the attraction, chemistry, and connection. I didn't question him
about the wisdom of going in again, I've been there. But you
might as well tell somebody they need open-heart surgery
to remove the person—they never listen. Think about it,
have you ever listened in similar circumstances?

Tom told me that all the love, yearning, and frustration
exploded in a beautiful night of making love and making
amends. They stayed up until dawn and Megan said she had
never stopped loving Tom, that he had never left her heart,
that she had never, with anybody else, felt a fraction of
what she felt with him. She had gotten her life together,
gotten into grad school, found her own place to live; she
felt ready.

Tom had heard her say the same thing so many times
before, only to have her disappear, that it was hard to believe her. He could see that she meant it fully in the moment, but then she left. And then she would come back
again after he had suffered mightily in her absence and was
just getting over her.

The 2004 Nobel Prize in theoretical physics was given
in a field called quantum chromodynamics: the study of
the subatomic particles called quarks, which are smaller
than protons and electrons. The closer quarks approach each
other, the weaker becomes their attraction to each other;
physicists call this attraction the "color force." When they

move apart, the force becomes stronger as the distance increases.

"This property may be compared to a rubber band," the Nobel Academy said. "The more the band is stretched, the stronger the force. The less it is stretched, the weaker the force."

This rubber-banding effect is not dissimilar to what happens in certain relationships. When the couple is apart, they yearn to be together. When they are together, like a limp rubber band, the force is weak.

This describes Tom and Megan to a T.

They had been through so much together—the heart-ache, the betrayal, the crazy-making—that Tom had begun to look at Megan as an unintentional teacher of the lesson of impermanence. She was here today and gone tomorrow. And every time he had an expectation of her behavior, she flipped it around, as consistent as a rubber band.

She also taught him many other unintentional lessons. Her extreme sensitivity taught Tom to be more gentle. Her inability to be available on his schedule taught him patience and how to back off his hard-charging style. Her fear forced Tom to look at his own resolve. Tom was fully looking at the relationship as a spiritual journey, even though they weren't in it very often. But, mostly, Megan seemed to be about teaching Tom the lesson of impermanence.

Three days had passed and a few passionate e-mails had been exchanged since their joyful reunion, when she called Tom.

"Hi, can we talk about things?"

"Sure," Tom said, recognizing what he called "the voice." The voice was whenever Megan had crawled up into her own head so far that her voice sounded as disembodied as the computer HAL in *2001*. No joy, no passion, no heart.

"I don't think I'm ready," Megan said. "I still need more time getting to know the most important person in my life, namely me. I haven't found out who I am yet."

"Oh God," Tom said. "I love the way you talk when you're about to give 'the speech.' You know, where you say you're not ready, haven't resolved an old relationship, love me dearly but don't want to engage in anything that might be a rip-off to both of us—blah, blah, blah."

Silence on the other end of the line.

"I don't mean to be completely flippant, but I've heard 'the speech' four times already." Tom was understandably losing his equanimity.

"I know, I know," Megan said. "I'm sorry, I just don't think I can do it."

"You know, I understand that," Tom said. "But I want *you* to understand something. You will always feel blown out by what we have together. It's intense and frightening."

"I think I might do better with something a little less intense or transcendent. Something a little more practical and ordinary."

"I have to say I don't understand the thinking behind 'it's too thrilling, so maybe I should play it safe,' " Tom said.

I do. Because if you lose somebody who isn't as much fun or so thrilling, somebody who doesn't make you feel so amazing, then if it ends it will be manageable. It won't be as devastating. It's a kind of preemptive strike against sadness. But happiness in life is where you can grab it. And so are the thrills.

"I'm afraid we don't share the same values around

money. I'm a saver, you spend every last cent you make. We are also both so much alike, who's going to be the practical one? And would you be willing to move to Santa Cruz? Because I know I don't want to live in L.A. again," she said to Tom on the phone. The words came out measured and devoid of emotion. It was the head taking over the heart, Tom told me later, reciting every gory detail.

"You are hilarious," Tom said to her. "You've got to figure out the financials, the marriage, where we're going to live, who's going to make the money, every last detail before you'll even agree to see me for a date. What happened to 'one day at a time'?"

She laughed, but quickly grew quiet. "I'm just not ready."

"If you want, I'll drive up and we can talk about it in person," Tom said. "I want you to say this looking in my eyes. Let's see if you can do it. Every time you've given me 'the speech,' it's been on the phone or in an e-mail or a letter. I want you to look me in the eye and tell me you don't want to see me again. Because that's what's at stake here."

"I can't do that, because it wouldn't be true," she said in a soft voice.

Aren't thoughts and conditioning and voices incredible in their ability to warp what our direct experience is telling us is amazing? Megan's fear, her addiction to infatuation, the wonderful feeling that she gets when comes back, the loneliness and deprivation and relief she feels when she leaves, are preventing her from getting to what's on the other side of commitment.

I understood Megan. We all want guarantees. But there are no guarantees. We only have today. In fact, we may not even have today. We only have right now. Better to look at a relationship the way you look at life, as a lifetime of NOWs.

There is no untangling that Gordian knot of fear. It comes from conditioning, and you can spend years and years figuring it out. But often the more you engage this knot, the more entangled and confused you get. Simply allow it to dissolve in the infinite NOW. Come fully into what you are doing in the moment, and let your physical reality ground you, whether driving your car or chopping vegetables for lunch. Pay no attention to the buzzing mind. Let it buzz, but don't feed it with your attention. Don't tell a story about it. Don't try to control it. Don't treat the negative mind as real. It is an illusion. It will evaporate like clouds in the hot sun if you pay it no mind.

Simply come to stillness and feel the love that is.

Of course, when Megan and Tom got together, that's not what they did. They went through every possible scenario. By the end of the night, they had covered it all, every fear, the issue of codependency, even Megan's confession that she felt she didn't know how to be loving. She knew how to *feel love* but had no idea how to express it in a loving way. She couldn't get out of herself.

By the end of the night, Tom and Megan were again moving forward. Who knows where it is going, or if it will survive the continuous scrutiny? Their relationship is like a record with a scratch in it. They hit the scratch in the middle of the first song and get bounced off. Months later they start over again, making beautiful music, the stylus easily finding its groove—until they hit the same scratch, the hiccup that scatters the music. Maybe beyond that one scratch lies an entire lifetime of rich and beautiful music waiting to be shared and explored. Maybe this time they will find it, moving beyond the fear.

Or maybe, tomorrow, Tom will be hearing "the speech."

Such is the nature of impermanence, Megan's special gift to Tom.

Someday his lesson may be to move on, to escape the labyrinth of their dynamic and be with somebody he can count on. Or maybe Megan and Tom will end up together, finally honoring the love and connection that is there. In reality, if the best indication of future behavior is past behavior, they might just keep going on like this for years.

Either way, as long as Tom looks at it as his spiritual lesson, his way to loosen his grip on what he thinks he needs to make him happy, then all will be fine. But as long as he tries to control the relationship or Megan, he is writing himself a prescription for suffering.

Tom, like all of us, can be free within the relationship or he can be free leaving the relationship. His freedom is within, only dependent upon how well he understands the impermanence of all things.

# CONNECTION

## Make the World Your Partner

Give love in the NOW—
it can't be given at any other time.

ARTHUR JEON

There are as many different permutations of love as there are people on the planet. And, in a way, it is like the old Indian folktale about five blind men who have been brought up to an elephant and asked to describe it.

"It is like a snake," says one, who is touching the elephant's trunk.

"No, it is like a tree," says another, with his arms around a thick leg.

"No, it is a wall, made of wood," said the third, hands flat on the elephant's side.

"It is a fan," cried the fourth, touching the elephant's ear.

"It's like none of those things," said the fifth man, who was holding the elephant's tail. "It is like a rope."

Obviously, from a relative point of view, they are all correct—they all have a subjective perception of the elephant—it is their direct experience. And yet, on an absolute level, none of them is correct because their perceptions and experience are incomplete.

And so it is with our experience of love. We are all blind (or at least wearing blinders), and we all experience love from the different perspectives of our conditioning. But it goes deeper than that. Although we are all completely different from each other, with different experiences that we bring to a relationship, there are certain things that are immutable.

Love, "the feeling," is a passive thing. Falling in love, feeling love, that is easy—an encounter with the right and rare combination of luck and chemistry, and voilà, you are "in love." I don't mean to denigrate this—it's a beautiful thing, filled with passion, thrills, and anxiety. It is the fuel that blasts the rocket of relationship into the stratosphere.

But learning how to *express love* and how to *be loving,* is an entirely different thing. It is a lifelong practice, which we all must commit ourselves to and learn how to do. It is a muscle that only grows strong and healthy with use. There is no preparation for love. If you don't use this muscle, it atrophies.

Like all emotions, love can only be expressed or felt in the moment. Don't latch on to the word "practice" here, as though if you practice enough, someday in the future you can finally be a loving human being. The only way to practice being loving is right NOW.

The other day I saw a homeless woman in a wheelchair, begging. She had a plastic cup with a few meager coins, which had tipped over onto the busy sidewalk. People were walking over the coins as she tried to reach down to the sidewalk to retrieve them. Then a girl stooped down and, without hesitation, began to pick up the coins.

"Let me help you, dear," she said to the old woman, who didn't reply, who in fact seemed to be completely out of it. The girl was kneeling at this old woman's feet, picking up the dirty coins, being jostled by pedestrians. When she stood up, she pulled a couple of coins out of her jeans and plopped them into the cup.

"Sorry it can't be more," she said lightly, before moving down the street. The old woman in the wheelchair never looked at her or acknowledged her in any way. Did this matter to the girl? I doubt it very much.

Was she in love with any particular person at that moment? Had she met the man of her dreams or "called in 'the one' " or was she in the middle of some insane sexual chemistry?

No. She was simply in the flow of love, moving moment by moment, giving love. She was compassionate to somebody who could do nothing for her. She wasn't giving to get, she was simply expressing her love.

The other day I took my friend's beloved dog, Babushka, on a hike in the Santa Monica Mountains. She is a little brown-nosed, bowlegged Staffordshire terrier with a heart of pure gold. She is so filled with love that she literally stops people walking down the street. She almost always elicits a smile from those who are awake enough to see her true nature. Some people, however, apparently think she's a pit bull and move out of her way like she was an electric eel that might shock them. In this way Babushka is a bit of a litmus test.

It was cloudy when we started to climb, but when we

got to the top of the overlook, the sun had come out and it was hot. Babushka went through the water quickly as I gave her drinks and wet her down to keep her cool. As we started down, the little dog was struggling and we were out of water. So I started asking people for water.

"Oh my God, of course," the first two women I asked said. "Here, take my bottle."

"Are you sure?" I asked. "Are you going to be all right?"

"We'll be fine," they both said together.

They were so generous and loving, and paused to hug and kiss Babushka.

The water went fast, and I asked a man walking up the trail with a large liter bottle of water for a bit of water for Babushka.

"This is all I have," he said without pausing, holding up his full bottle. I looked at Babushka, who was panting, with her tongue lolling out of her head, the very picture of thirst. I sighed. I couldn't believe he could ignore a dog in need like this. I felt anger at him, and anger at myself for not planning better.

And so it went down the mountain, cadging water all the way. I must have asked ten people, of whom six gave willingly and four did not. And I got to thinking that this was exactly what love was like. It is water and sustenance, and most of us are like Babushka, walking with our tongues hanging out, wishing for a few drops. Some people give it away freely, and others hoard it.

But life is like that hike up and down that mountain. We encounter people in need, and we are sometimes in need ourselves. And I noticed that it was difficult for me to ask for help—I'm used to being emotionally self-sufficient. If it was for me, I probably would have died of thirst on that mountain before asking for help. But for Babushka I would have done anything. Why? Because the love of an animal is unconditional. If you rescue a little animal from the pound, you are under the impression that you are rescuing them, when in reality they are rescuing you in every way that is important. They love you unconditionally and they need you unconditionally. They give you an opportunity to be unconditionally loving, one of the most important gifts one living being can give another. They prime the pump of your own wellspring of love.

Those who ignored us in our need on that mountain were not awake to the suffering of the tiny dog. Starting out, I was not awake to the fact that it was a warm day. We are all like that at times: not awake. There are times in the world when you will be without a partner. There are times when you feel very far from ever finding a partner. There are lonely times when you feel at best disconnected from the rest of the world and at worst like some kind of unlovable freak. But that doesn't have to preclude your wakefulness.

A married friend of mine just told me the story of a woman, a colleague he worked with on a project, who was expressing interest in him. She was unmarried and in her mid-thirties. My friend, for reasons of circulation in his hands, doesn't wear a wedding ring. Before he told the woman that he was married, she was charming and fascinated and interested in everything he had to say. When he told her that he was married, with two children, the woman simply turned it off. She became completely uninterested in my friend as a human being and as a potential friend— she was only interested in him as a potential partner.

"She was missing out on a potentially great friendship, because we really got along," my friend said. "Not to mention all sorts of career synergy and introductions to all my single friends."

But the woman had an agenda. When my friend didn't fit into it, she moved on.

We have all been there.

But instead of waiting for love to show up in the form of your dream man or woman, instead of pining away in existential loneliness, try this instead:

Drop your identification with your story that you need love from outside.

Witness your thoughts as a product of your conditioning.

Know that you need nothing to experience love.

All you need to do is move through the world, moment by moment.

Awake to the possibility of expressing love.

And then give it to every living being you encounter.

Do it for an hour and see if it changes your mood.

Increase the time you are in this loving awareness.

Notice that the loneliness has disappeared.

That people are flocking to you.

That your heart is full.

Now release the idea that there is even an "I" that is doing this.

Get rid of the idea of yourself as a "person who loves," and simply love. The only way to do this is to drop the identification with "me."

Once the small self disappears, it reveals a connection with the big self.

It is the act of love that is transformative.

Partner with the world, love all that is.

# About the Author

ARTHUR JEON leads Dharma Conversations and teaches yoga at Yoga Works in Santa Monica, California. He is the author of *City Dharma: Keeping Your Cool in the Chaos*. Visit him at www.sexloveanddharma.com and www.citydharma.com.

## KEEPING YOUR COOL
## IN THE CHAOS

*City Dharma* teaches you how to keep your cool even when
the road to enlightenment leads you straight through
downtown at rush hour.

1-4000-4909-1
$12.95 paper (Canada: $17.95)
Wherever books are sold

Three Rivers Press
CrownPublishing.com

"This witty, wise, anecdote-filled examination of the perils and possibilities of pursuing the spiritual path is an entertaining, illuminating read."
>—*Yoga Journal*

"Hip, smart, urban, and funny—a new voice for the dharma that lives in the city."
>—Catherine Ingram, author of
>*Passionate Presence*

"A manual of contemplations to get you through the urban elements that wreak havoc on your soul."
>—*New York Daily News*

"Straightforward, sensitive, and sassy, Jeon's approach offers effective methods for turning down that annoying voice in your head from a wail to a whisper."
>—*Booklist*

"This timely book is very relevant to our current concerns in the here and now, as well as our connection with the timeless verities."
>—Lama Surya Das, author of
>*Awakening the Buddha Within*